SNOWDEN SLIGHTS,
WILDFOWLER.

BY

SYDNEY H. SMITH.

*With Illustrations from photographs
by the Author.*

British Library Cataloguing-in-Publication Data
A catalogue record for this book is available from the
British Library

Shooting Wildfowl

Wildfowl hunting or shooting is the practice of hunting ducks, geese, quail or other wildfowl for food and sport. In many western countries, commercial wildfowl hunting is prohibited, and sub-genres such as duck hunting have become sporting activities. Many types of ducks and geese share the same habitat, have overlapping or identical hunting seasons, and are hunted using the same methods. Thus, it is possible to take different species of wildfowl in the same outing – waterfowl are by far the most commonly hunted birds though. Waterfowl can be hunted in crop fields where they feed, or, more frequently, on or near bodies of water such as rivers, lakes, ponds, swamps, sloughs, or oceanic coastlines.

Wild wildfowl have been hunted for food, down and feathers worldwide, since prehistoric times. Ducks, geese, and swans appear in European cave paintings from the last Ice Age, and a mural in the Ancient Egyptian tomb of Khum-Hotpe (c. 1900 BC) shows a man in a hunting blind (a covering device for trackers) capturing swimming ducks in a trap. Wildfowl hunting proper - with shotguns - only began in the seventeenth century with the invention of the matchlock shotgun. Later flintlock shotguns and percussion cap guns have also been used, but in general shotguns have been loaded with black powder and led shots, through the muzzle, right up until the late nineteenth century. The history of shooting wildfowl is very much tied up with the development of the shotgun. It was the semi-automatic 12 ga. gun, developed by John Browning in the very early twentieth century which allowed hunters to shoot on a large, commercial scale. Once wildfowlers (primarily in America and Europe) had access to such guns, they could become much more proficient market hunters. They used a four-shell magazine (five including the one in the chamber) to rake rafts of ducks on the water or to shoot them at night in order to kill larger numbers of birds. Even during the great depression years, a brace of Canvasbacks could easily be sold, but legislation was gradually brought in to prevent such practices.

Early European settlers in America hunted the native birds with great zeal, as the supply of wildfowl, especially waterfowl on the coastal Atlantic regions seemed endless. During the fall migrations, the skies were filled with birds. Locations such as Chesapeake Bay, Delaware Bay and Barnaget Bay were hunted extensively. As more immigrants came to America in the late eighteenth and nineteenth centuries, the need for more food became greater. Market hunting started to take form, to supply the local population living along the Atlantic coast with fresh ducks and geese. Men would go into wooden boats and go out into the bays hunting, sometimes with large shotguns – and they could bring back one or two barrels of ducks each day. Live ducks were used as decoys, as well as bait such as corn or grain to attract other wildfowl.

There are several items used by almost all wildfowl hunters: a shotgun, ammunition, a hunting blind, decoys, a boat (if needed), and various bird calls. The decoys are used to lure the birds within range, and the blind conceals the hunter. When a hunter or hunters sees the wildfowl, he or she begins calling with an appropriate bird-call. Once the birds are within range, the hunters rise from the blind and quickly shoot them before they are frightened off and out of shooting range. Duck or goose calls are often used to attract birds, but sometimes calls of other birds are simulated to convince the birds that there is no danger. Today, due to the ban on lead shots for hunting wildfowl over wetlands, many wildfowlers are switching to modern guns with stronger engineering to allow the use of non-toxic ammunition such as steel or tungsten based cartridges. The most popular bore is the 12-gauge. Only certain 'quarry' species of wildfowl may legally be shot in the UK, and are protected under the Wildlife and Countryside Act 1981. These are Mallard, Wigeon, Teal, Pochard, Shoveler, Pintail, Gadwall, Goldeneye, Tufted Duck, Canada Goose, White-fronted Goose, Greylag Goose and Pink-footed Goose. Other common quarry targets for the wildfowler include the Common Snipe.

An intimate knowledge of the quarry and its habitat is required by the successful wildfowler. Shooting will normally occur during the early morning and late afternoon 'flights', when the birds move to and from feeding and roosting sites. A long way from the market hunters of the eighteenth century, current wildfowlers do not search for a large bag of quarry; their many hours efforts can be well-rewarded by even a single bird. Wildfowling has come under threat in recent years through legislation though. Destruction of habitat also has played a large part in the decline of shooting areas, and recently in the UK 'right to roam' policies mean that wildfowlers' conservation areas are at risk. However, in most regions, good relationships exist between wildfowlers, conservationists, ramblers and other coastal area users. In America, the situation is rather different, due to the concerted efforts of J.N. Darling in the 1930s. He urged the government to pass the 'Migratory Bird Hunting Stamp Act' better known as the 'Federal Duck Stamp Act', which required hunters to purchase a special stamp, in addition to a regular hunting license, to hunt migratory waterfowl. This scheme has funded the purchase of 4.5 million acres of National Wildlife Refuge land since its inception in 1934. The Duck Stamp act has been described as 'one of the most successful conservation programs ever devised.' Thanks to such efforts, which maintain the natural habitats of wildfowl, and especially of waterfowl, the sport is still enjoyed by many, all over the world.

BURBERRY WEATHERPROOF SHOOTING KIT.

Reliably Protective. Airylight. Healthful.

The Wildfowler, clad in BURBERRY is insured against the ill-effects of wet, cold, and all weather vicissitudes, whilst retaining the freedom from restraint to limb and muscle which is essential to good shooting and comfort.

Illustrated
Catalogue
and
Patterns
Post Free.

Every
Genuine
Burberry
Garment is
Labelled
Burberry

The Burberry,

splendid safeguard for winter punt and flight-shooting. Proof against wet penetration, warm, airylight and easy fitting. Neutral colourings tone with surroundings and are practically invisible.

BURBERRYS Haymarket, S.W., LONDON;

Boul. Malesherbes, PARIS; and Provincial Agents.

SNOWDEN SLIGHTS.

PREFACE.

My principal object in compiling this brief sketch of the life and craft of that fine old character, Snowden Slights, of East Cottingwith, in the County of Yorkshire, better known, perhaps, as the "Last of the Yorkshire Wildfowlers," has been to set down in black and white such reminiscences concerning himself and his almost unique methods of wildfowling, together with some account of his success as a fisherman and "handy man" generally, as would be of interest to all lovers of sport, and at the same time to give to the public a permanent record of the vivid personality and marvellous resource of this grand old son of the North.

I have known the old wildfowler for two-thirds of my life ; true, as yet that life cannot be called a long one, but the time has sufficed to enable me to form an intimate appreciation of his many admirable qualities. I have accompanied him in both rough and smooth weather, and on scores of occasions I have had my feet under the same table. I claim, therefore, to know him intimately and sympathetically, and this must constitute my apology for placing before the public another book dealing so largely with the somewhat hackneyed subject of wildfowling. Many of my photographs have appeared previously in the various sporting publications, and I must express my indebtedness for the loan of blocks to A. E. T. Watson, Esq., Editor of "The Badminton Magazine" ; P. Anderson Graham, Esq., Editor of "Country Life" ; the Editor of "The County Gentleman" ; G. J. Maddick, Esq., Editor of "The Illustrated Sporting and Dramatic News" ; A. C. Bonsall, Esq., of "The Shooting

Times" ; Wm. Hill, Esq., of "The Gamekeepers' Gazette" ; and to the Editor of "The Gamekeeper." Also for the two excellent drawings of wild duck, and flight shooting at wild duck, which are by Mr. Stanley Duncan, the well-known sporting writer.

In writing the chapter on the Derwent Valley I have referred to the excellent short history of the district written by Mr. Tom Bradley, for the Derwent, in the sketch map of the river published by "The Yorkshire Weekly Post." Where I have made reference to Mr. Nelson's monograph on "The Birds of Yorkshire," I have inserted a note to that effect.

My thanks are specially due to my friend Mr. Chas. F. Procter, Vice-President of The Wildfowlers' Association of Great Britain and Ireland, for his labours in reading the proofs, and for many hints which have proved of considerable value. I also desire to thank Oxley Grabham, Esq., M.A., Curator of the York Museum, for his kindness in correcting the proofs of the chapter dealing with the birds of the Derwent Valley.

S. H. S.

YORK, 1912.

CONTENTS.

SNOWDEN
SLIGHTS'
COTTAGE AT
EAST
COTTINGWITH.

LIST OF ILLUSTRATIONS

SYDNEY H. SMITH.

THE BIG GUN IS A HEAVY LOAD.

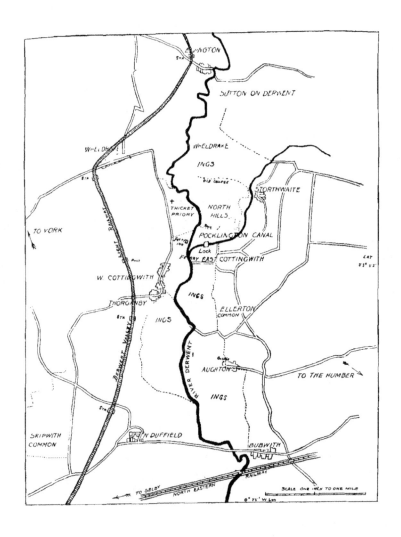

SNOWDEN SLIGHTS IN 1910.

SNOWDEN SLIGHTS, WILDFOWLER.

CHAPTER I.

INTRODUCTORY.

THE art of wildfowling is as old as the hills. It has survived from the time when primitive man pitted his skilfully contrived snares against the cunning of the wild geese and ducks and myriads of lesser fowl which once swarmed over these islands.

The march of science has in no wise nullified the art of wildfowling, for along with the strides made in the invention of more deadly lethal weapons, and our greater knowledge of the natural history of our quarry, the wariness of the feathered tribe has kept pace in proportionate degree.

Every winter immense flocks of wild geese descend upon our shores from their icy fastnesses in the far North, and the early spring sees the return of these again, hardly a whit the worse for their hot reception along our inhospitable shores. Every sporting newspaper heralds the first appearance of them; by telegraph and post their progress down the coast is anticipated, and their advent

I   A prepared for. Wildfowlers are in wait to welcome (?) them, armed with the most deadly sinews of war that modern skill and ingenuity can devise—specially-built wild-fowl guns, shooting heavy charges of shot—carefully-designed punts with huge breech-loading guns fitted on the very latest types of mount and recoil gear. All is in readiness to exact toll from the ranks of the wariest of God's creatures, and with what result? I venture to say not one per cent. of the quarry is annually brought to bag.

I cannot overlook the effect of evolution upon such species as wild swans, ducks, and many of the more sought-after and larger waders. Our forbears with their primitive methods of capture, of necessity took toll only of those birds which were the most confiding, leaving the more wary to propagate their race. It is therefore evident that as time went on higher types would be evolved, and we have to-day flocks of fowl more cunning than of yore, and from which, to a certain extent, we ourselves eliminate those which are the least "spry."

There is a lot of ink spilled concerning the decrease in the numbers of wildfowl, some of it, no doubt, justly. In my humble opinion, it is far more probable that the fowl are merely driven to seek fresh quarters. At the present day there are ten times the number of shooters there were twenty years ago, the acreage of marshy, attractive local-ities has shrunk enormously during the same period, and if we frighten the wildfowl by a never-ending fusillade of powder and shot, and also destroy their natural haunts by draining fen-lands, reclaiming saltings and foreshores, and by building docks and shipyards on the estuaries which the wildfowl have frequented from time immemorial, it is only in the natural order of events that they will have to go farther afield in search of another place where they can find a plentiful supply of food, and an immunity from danger.

As a naturalist and sportsman, I deplore the passing of the fowl from their old haunts, but I recognise the claims of mankind as being beyond that of the birds. Provision must be made for an expanding population, and the very progress of knowledge and civilisation that drives away the wildfowl, supplies us with the means of transport to follow them into the new solitudes they are invading.

There is a regular immigration of wildfowl into this country every winter, and a regular emigration out of it again in the spring, but it is only certain localities that attract the fowl in any numbers. Their numbers appear to vary in cycles, a great profusion sometimes occurring after several seasons of scarcity. This phenomenon is difficult to intelligently account for. Weather is a heavy factor in deciding these immigrations, and in a later chapter I shall have occasion to point out instances. Severe winters farther North inevitably mean the driving south of larger flocks of wildfowl, and should hard weather continue any length of time, the birds that have taken up a temporary abode in our neighbourhood will, naturally, move southward again in quest of food, which, after all, is the prime motive ruling all movements amongst wild fauna.

After the foregoing remarks, I will revert to the main object I had in view when I first took up my pen. As far as the Derwent Valley is concerned, the art of wildfowling with punt and gun made its debut about four generations ago, when one Richard Bell, of East Cottingwith, followed the pursuit of "wilde fowles." About 1830, John Slights, of Pocklington, was appointed schoolmaster at East Cottingwith, and probably because he had often watched Bell push boldly out in his frail punt, in quest of the ducks that swarmed in immense numbers over the flooded Derwent Valley, he took up wildfowling as a hobby. Apparently in his day, a little learning went a long way. To take up his mastership, he had left the thriving business of a fish and game dealer ; no doubt his inside knowledge of the latter part of his trade would eventually stand him in good stead, although he has left no records behind him of which we might judge. He taught the young idea in this village school, and incidentally augmented his income by wildfowling, until about 1845, when at the age of sixty-six, he received the call to which there can be no deaf ear, leaving behind him a family of three sons and five daughters.

It is most unfortunate that he left no notes of the many interesting things which must have come under his notice ; being a man of considerable intelligence, his remarks would have been of great value to present-day fowlers and ornithologists.

His second son, Snowden, born in July, 1830, gave promise at an early age of becoming an expert fowler. He commenced his sporting education coincident with leaving school, and at the tender age of nine years. In the winter months, he went out regularly with his father in the punt, and evinced such a liking for the sport, and an aptitude for the gun, that he was left pretty much to his own devices, with the result that by the time he had attained his fifteenth birthday he had become quite proficient in shooting. The rough life he had led helped considerably in moulding him into a man, and at fifteen his looks greatly belied his years. A weedy youth would have been quite unable to trudge about with the long-barrelled single muzzle-loading gun that was his weapon.

JOHN SLIGHTS. FATHER OF SNOWDEN.

SKET-MAKING
Slights is the
central figure.

In the summer months he worked casually for the local farmers, ran errands for his father, or filled up his spare time in the kitchen-garden, or in hanging about the door of the village workshop, where some basket-makers plied their calling. When the time arrived for him definitely to settle on his life's vocation, he decided to adopt that of a basket-maker. He had so often watched the men as they dexterously wove the supple osiers into varied shapes and styles of baskets, that he felt confident he could emulate their example. His proper course would have been to apprentice himself in the shop wherein he had so often idled, but no, he must commence work unaided, and by constant application alone, he won through, and established his own little shop.

As the winters came round, he did not allow the pursuit of wildfowling to lapse, but followed the sport diligently for its own sake, and also for a livelihood. In order to save the cost of carriage on ducks destined for the market, he tramped into Pocklington once, and sometimes twice a week, a distance of about nine miles each way. On one of these visits he met his future wife, and there married her when he had attained his majority. He took up his abode permanently at East Cottingwith, and for a few years his life was singularly hard. However, he struggled on bravely, and although he often went short of food, so that he could raise sufficient money to pay his rent, he did not complain, but kept on hoping for better times. He laid out the whole of his minute capital in some osier patches. Osiers are fairly profitable when well grown, but as they take about three years to reach a marketable value, it sometimes happens that the cultivator with straitened resources cannot afford to wait until they have reached

their full maturity. The time to cut the beds had almost
arrived when there came a long spell of bad weather, and
his troubles culminated, when one day the ice which gripped
the river and adjacent flooded "ings" broke up, and, borne
on the crest of the rising flood, crashed destructively over
the carefully-kept plantings, so that in a few moments
the result of several years of patient labour was utterly
destroyed.

For a time the poor fellow was almost beside himself at
his loss, but the old proverb, "It is an ill wind that blows
nobody any good," justified itself in this case. The big
floods attracted huge flocks of wildfowl which perforce
paid toll to the now skilful fowler, whose punt left home
at dusk, returning with its half-frozen, lonely occupant in
the cold, grey hours, laden gunwale-deep with goose, and
swan, and duck, in numbers we latter-day exponents of the
art deem well-nigh incredible. Honest as daylight, and,
above all, a sportsman, who scorned to take a mean advantage of his quarry, in spite of the fact of its being his
"daily bread," his sterling qualities soon found recognition
amongst the county families of the neighbourhood. To-day
his eye kindles at the mention of Lord Wenlock, and Mr.
J. J. Dunnington Jefferson, portions of whose estates are
annually flooded with water, attracting innumerable wildfowl, and who have privileged Snowden Slights, even as
their forbears did his father, to launch his grim, grey and
shadowy punt into the misty expanses, where a kaleidoscopic
throng of restless and wary creatures disport themselves.

The art of Snowden Slights has had its imitators along
the course of the Derwent Valley. Punts have been
launched from Duffield, Ellerton, and Bubwith, but in no
case has the experiment met with much success, probably

more through lack of application than actual want of skill on the part of the would-be fowlers. A puntsman, named Laverack, occasionally went out from Duffield, and Thomas Barnard essayed his luck from the tiny hamlet of Ellerton, while Bubwith was represented by a schoolmaster, Thomas Ross, and a bricklayer, appropriately named George Hodd, the last two following the sport merely as a hobby. Another wildfowling season has come, and will have gone, ere these lines appear in print, but the old fowler is still hale and hearty. True, his limbs are not so supple, nor is his eye so keen—four-score years have whitened his hair and lined his features, but an indomitable spirit still pervades his being, and he will not admit his fowling days are over. Like a gnarled old oak he defies the wintry blast, until his cronies good-naturedly suggest he will have to stop a charge of shot from his own big gun, before he departs to the happy hunting-grounds.

Last of the Yorkshire wildfowlers, when he lays aside his gun, his art dies with him. Other members of his family (there are three generations of them), have essayed to follow in his footsteps, but only one with any hope of success, his grandson, Snowden Plaxton, a six-foot four-inch Yorkshireman, with a fist like a shoulder of mutton and the heart of a child. He was a wildfowler of golden promise, but was unfortunately thrown from his horse when serving with the troop of Yeomanry to which he belonged, and when, after months of suffering he was laid to rest, the hopes of the old wildfowler that he would leave a successor were buried in the grave.

Snowden Slights is of a type nowadays far too scarce— a fine sportsman, a kindly, good-natured, honest, and generous man—I am better for having known him. He has given me many wrinkles about the habits of his quarry, and his methods in securing them.   He has many friends, few enemies (I trust, none), the world is better for his having lived, and will surely be the poorer for his departure.

CHAPTER II.

SUMMER AND WINTER VOCATION.

T HE craft of the basket-maker dates back to the time
when the ancient Briton dyed his body with woad to
serve in lieu of clothes, and sailed out upon the
waters to catch fish before he could partake of his
breakfast. The cockleshell boat, or "coracle," in which he
ventured forth was woven from the wild growing osiers—a
frail, skilfully constructed thing of basket work, covered with
the skins of animals which his hunter's craft had procured
him. Whether it is that Snowden Slights has inherited any
latent talent in this direction from one of his long-past
progenitors, I know not. Be that as it may, Slights—as I
have already remarked—early adopted the calling of a
basket-maker.

Land suitable for osier-growing was then both plentiful
and cheap (in fact, much of it in the district is unsuited
to grow anything else), and during the spring and early
summer, our friend was busy cultivating the supple stems,
cutting and weaving them from early morn until dewy eve.
There was a continuous brisk demand for market baskets,
potato skips, and many others of various sizes and shapes,
and as long as a good supply of osiers could be procured,
there was plenty of work ready to hand. Those who pursue
the calling of a basket-maker (leaving out of account the

9

workers regularly employed by large firms) generally lead a nomadic life, and Slights was able to give employment to several of the wandering followers of his craft. During middle age, therefore, Slights was in receipt of a fairly good income, but not possessing any penchant for saving his spare cash, he has had abundant opportunity in later years to regret his earlier lack of forethought.

The work of a basket-maker is hard—in fact, very laborious ; on the other hand, as skilled workmen are scarce, wages are good to really efficient craftsmen. Then, too, it is a healthy business, being principally carried on in the open air, far away from the congested area of our towns, and the only reason I can see for there not being more followers of the profession is, that no system of apprenticeship pertains, with the result that very little fresh blood is imported. A journeyman basket-maker has usually picked up the trade from casual employment, or he is a broken-down employer, whose craving for drink has destroyed his business, and driven him out to roam the countryside. Such is the man who will take a few weeks' regular work in the potato season, and turn out "Pickers" baskets by the score, and as soon as he has worked his job up, will draw his pay, and settle at the nearest public-house until he has swallowed every penny of his hard-earned money. With these remarks I will dismiss this rather uninteresting subject of basket-making, and turn to the winter vocation of wildfowling.

The love of sport is deeply ingrained in every man, though we do not all find an outlet for it, but should the call come to us, we generally respond in haste, lest the chance go by. Snowden Slights was reared in an atmosphere of sport. The ceiling of the little cottage in which he spent his early life literally bristled with hooks, from which hung suspended a weird and wonderful array of guns, some small and many large, all of them from time to time being called into use by his father. Small wonder, indeed, was it that he had imbibed a love of sport, and more particularly that of wildfowling. Indeed, at the age of eighty it was evident to all that he was as engrossed in the subject as he had been half a century earlier.

At the approach of winter, there was usually a gradual slackening in the basket-making business ; the intervening time from then to the actual flooding of the Ings and the arrival of the wildfowl was consequently occupied in furbishing up his armoury, caulking and painting the gun-punts, and generally making ready for sport, and providing against the hardships of the winter months. To be a successful wildfowler, one must first of all possess an iron constitution, and, secondly, a complete knowledge of the habits and peculiarities of the hundred and one varieties of wildfowl with which you may be brought into contact. Other aids to success are—a cheerful disposition an aptitude for expeditiously extricating oneself from perilous positions, and for the taking of speedy advantage of opportunities which may present themselves. It is hardly necessary to say that Snowden Slights has more than fulfilled all these requirements, and has thus become the grand old sportsman we know him to be to-day.

For the benefit of those who do not know what wildfowling really is, a little explanation may not be out of place here :—Wildfowling is the snaring, netting or shooting of all the different species of birds that may be designated by the title of wildfowl. Of course, the term might be applied to ALL wild birds, but it is generally limited to those having either an edible value, or as affording a special form of sport to the disciples of Nimrod. Roughly, there are about half-a-dozen species of wild geese, two of wild swans, and fifteen respectively of ducks and waders, making approximately a total of thirty-eight kinds which come within the category of true wildfowl as the legitimate prey of the wild-fowler, and this out of the odd three hundred and eighty species of birds which figure on the British list.

As far as the PROFESSIONAL wildfowler is concerned, the foregoing list may again be considerably reduced, but as I shall have occasion in a future chapter to mention in detail those birds which more particularly concern the professional, I need not go further with this analysis. Having graduated in the school of actuality, Slights possessed the faculty of being able to foretell what kind of weather would be likely to ensue during certain seasons of sport, and this was of great help in arranging his excursions in quest of fowl. Given certain conditions of wind, frost, or blizzard, of rough or smooth, the ducks would arrive from this or that direction, and would make for definite portions of his territory. His skill as a weather prophet naturally reduced his hard work, and such good judgment often enabled him to leave his punt and gun several miles away from home, well knowing he would be able to return in the late afternoon or early morning, as the case might be, and be almost sure to obtain a shot; and as this procedure would perchance save him making a long and arduous detour or difficult paddle, the advantage is apparent.

I have often proved the old man's accuracy in forecasting the exact line of an evening flight. My own knowledge of the locality would often cause me to select a stand, but with an apology for his correction, Slights would suggest moving

PUNT SHOOTING
—TAKING AIM.

READY TO PULL
THE TRIGGER.

another hundred yards, to right or left, and invariably his selection proved to be amply justified. The pursuit of wild-fowl has caused his life to be one long round of cold and exposure. Winter after winter has he endured the vigorous test of the elements ; the lines have deepened in his face, his figure has shrunk, but his back is still straight, and his eyes keen, and the spell of Nature still hangs over him. The winter vocation of Snowden Slights was to him a necessity, not only as a means of earning a livelihood, but as a sport. The charm grew upon him as surely as that of gambling does upon the would-be bank-breaker at Monte Carlo, until he was quite obsessed in his daily quest.

His enthusiasm may be judged from the following instances. During a hard winter, there came one Saturday evening when every condition of weather appeared favour-able, a windless eve, accompanied by frost, yet not quite keen enough to seal all the open water in its icy grip. There was a big company of wildfowl on the glassy expanse, and everything pointed to a most successful expedition. So it was in a very cheerful mood that the old man boarded his punt, and set out to encompass the destruction of all and sundry wildfowl of which he could get within shot. In spite, however, of all his efforts, his knowledge of their habits, and his skill with punt and gun, the fowl seemed more cunning than he had ever known them, and refused to allow the near approach of the punt. He passed the night in fruitless endeavour, and returned home to spend Sunday in meditation. Monday morning found him "up and doing," once more he set out to try conclusions with the birds ; again he was disappointed. All night was taken up in another bootless chase, and the week was spent in alternately returning home to snatch a few hours' sleep and necessary food, and in struggling to outmatch his elusive quarry. Though foiled on every hand, it was not until the following Saturday evening that he gave up the quest. He had never fired one shot—he had spent the week in entire solitude—every day wet to the skin, his clothes frozen upon him—half-dead from want of food and rest, and almost in tears with disappointment. He stumbled over the threshold of his home nearly paralysed with cold and fatigue, and after being assisted to the fire, thawed, and refreshed, he turned in and slept the clock round. So strong, however, was the passion of sport upon him, that within a few more hours he had sallied forth again, and this time the Fates were kind. Within half a mile of his home, he bagged about fourteen duck at one shot from his big gun. The old wildfowler does not recommend the vocation as a means of earning a living ; the life, he declares, is full of hardship, though also full of charm. At best, he says, it is a precarious method of ensuring a bare existence, and is not to be taken up seriously by anybody, but only as a hobby—one of the finest, certainly, that can be chosen. That it makes a man, is exemplified in the character I have described ; and as a winter vocation it is not to be commended, but, says Snowden Slights, "If I had my life to come over again, I would be a wildfowler, but I would go in for it properly" ; I often wonder what would have happened if "he had gone in for wildfowling properly"?

CHAPTER III.

THE DERWENT VALLEY.

ALTHOUGH this chapter is headed "The Derwent Valley," I propose to deal only with that portion of it which immediately concerns our subject, namely, the district adjoining the little village of East Cottingwith. Roughly speaking, it is bounded on the south by Bubwith, and on the north by Sutton Lock. The villages in this area are: Storwood, East and West Cottingwith, Thorganby, Elloughton, Aughton and Driffield. The Derwent rises on Wykeham High Moor, and after following a lengthy and very erratic course, empties itself into the Ouse at Barmby and Long Drax.

Close to its source, it receives a large number of contributory streams, and as these latter drain a very wide and elevated area, the main river is liable to sudden "freshes," which rush down its course in far heavier volume than can possibly be contained within the comparatively narrow channel of the lower reaches. The result is—the constant flooding of the low-lying country, and more particularly that below Sutton. This state of affairs has existed for hundreds of years, and is commented upon by a *writer who flourished about the middle of the sixteenth

_____

(*) Leland.

15

century. The river Derwent being tidal as far as Sutton Lock—this point being rather over seventy miles from the sea—the formation of mud and sand banks is thereby accelerated, as owing to the length of its channel, the warpy matter washed down by floods is never carried completely out of the river, but is dropped within the area in question, and annually helps to make matters worse, so far as floods are concerned. Practically every winter the river overflows its banks, and converts the low-lying "ings," or water-meadows, into a miniature freshwater sea, the section enclosed by the villages previously mentioned, varying in width from a quarter of a mile to a mile and a half and in length from fifteen to twenty miles. Previous to 1703, the Derwent was tidal, and for vessels of shallow draught navigable almost to Stamford Bridge, but about that date, powers of Parliament were obtained, and the river made navigable up to Malton, a scheme which necessitated the construction of five locks, and which opened up about fifty miles of the river from its mouth. The navigation rights were the property of Earl Fitzwilliam, but when the North-Eastern Railway opened the district up by railway construction, they purchased the navigation rights, and discouraged traffic over it. In a perfunctory sort of way, vessels still ply along its course, and some little water-borne business is done in agricultural material, stone for the repairs of roads and conveyance of coals. The possibilities of the Derwent are many, and if the Canal Commission ever sits to consider them, the result of their deliberations may mean the dredging of the channels, the prevention of floods, and the destruction of the wildfowling, which as yet may still be obtained by those who are so fortunately placed as to be able to enjoy it. That portion of the Derwent Valley with which we are concerned, is up to the present almost cut off from civilisation, which, of course, accounts for the presence of wildfowl within its limits. A railway connects its lower end, the nearest station to East Cottingwith being six miles away, while to reach the nearest town of any importance, one would have to journey by shanks' pony, cycle, or carrier's cart, ten miles to sleepy old York. There is little of interest to attract the tourist, and strangers are consequently quite a rarity ; a wide area of this portion of Yorkshire is very flat, and except to the naturalist or sportsman quite uninteresting, and the natives lead a humdrum life, tilling the fields, and retiring to bed when the daylight fails.

I have heard that some few stay out late at night, and devote the time in the pleasant occupation of catching sundry stray hares, apparently homeless rabbits, or knocking a pheasant on the head, if that noble bird happened to be occupying valuable space for its roosting-place in a tree. But I will not venture to vouch for the accuracy of the report. In the neighbourhood, there are the ruins of Wressle Castle, pretty much in the same condition as they were left by Oliver Cromwell after he had devoted a little time to his favourite occupation of bombarding such private strongholds. Aughton was the birthplace of the famous Robert Aske, the leader of the Pilgrimage of Grace, and in the ancient church there are monuments of himself and his wife, the arms of the family being carved on the old tower. At Ellerton, or Ellaughton, there are but a few remnants of stained glass in the windows of the church of St. Mary, which are supposed to have belonged to an old Gilbertine priory that once stood there. Thicket Priory stands upon the site of a Benedictine priory, founded somewhere about

B

1190, during the reign of Richard I. Probably it caught Cromwell's eye at the time he devoted a little attention to Wressle Castle ; at any rate, there is no vestige of it at the present day. If not very attractive to the ordinary tourist, the district draws numerous disciples of Izaak Walton from the crowded West Riding, and occasionally they are to be seen by the hundred "pegged down" along each bank, when some great event in the angling world has to be decided. To a certain extent the angling attractions of the lower reaches of the Derwent have passed away, chiefly as the result of the indiscriminate netting of the fish by local residents, and the taking of small fish by Waltonians, who ought to have known better. The Yorkshire Fishery Board do a good work in limiting the season during which fish may be taken, but they have a huge district to attend to, and it is an open secret in the Derwent Valley that anyone can have fish for dinner if they can get into touch with the right parties and stand them a pint of nut-brown ale. The Pocklington Canal connects with the Derwent at East Cottingwith ; it is also controlled by the North-Eastern Railway Company, and, owing to the discouragement of traffic long ago by the railway authorities, to-day it would be almost impossible to take a loaded vessel into the canal, and it is practically given up to one of the York angling clubs, who endeavour strictly to preserve the coarse fishing. The Canal once swarmed with large bream and pike, besides quantities of other coarse fish, but of late years the fishing has not been anything like so good as it was, although good catches are still occasionally made. The Pocklington Canal is only nine miles in length, and was constructed about 1814, and necessitated a lock to every mile of its short stretch. It forms a boundary on the top side of Wheldrake Ings, the quietest, largest, and best portion of the whole district as far as wildfowling is concerned, and to stand upon its southern bank on some clear frosty winter's day, and look up the river towards Sutton, one is greeted by a large expanse of water, stretching as far as the eye can see, dotted with ones, two's, small packs and flocks of many species of wildfowl, amongst which there is a preponderance of mallard (common wild duck).

Quite recently I estimated the number of wild duck of various species in sight to be from eight to ten hundred, and this appears to be a fair average, except during stress of weather, when the flocks are augmented by fresh arrivals from the coast, and then the wild waste of waters becomes literally covered with birds.

Slights remembers one hard winter in the "fifties" when his father estimated the wildfowl in sight to number over ten thousand. The banks of the river are very high, and at intervals strong "cloughs" are pierced in it, not only for the purpose of keeping back high spring tides from flooding the low land, but also to drain away the water from the "Ings" whenever the river falls low enough to permit of it, and, of course, when floods have made it necessary. Snowden Slights, privileged by the lords of the manor, operates these "cloughs" to flood the land at his discretion, but only during that part of the year when the low land is too sodden to be of any value except for wildfowling. It does not often happen that we have a dry winter, but when it does occur it becomes necessary to await a time when the river is higher than the Ings, and then to flood them by the aid of the bank "cloughs." But this is usually only done in the Wheldrake Ings, and a piece locally termed North Hills, but abbreviated to "Nor Hills." The lower section of the Derwent Valley appears to be mid-way of the flight-line of wildfowl, from the back of Yorkshire to the Humber estuary. One day there are immense flocks of birds in the Ings, the next, hardly any. Sometimes these wandering packs will stay several days, maybe several weeks, their movements are most uncertain, and it is impossible to tell what are the influences which dominate them.

It is well known that climatic conditions are the chief governing factors, but it sometimes occurs that early one morning the place will be found to be teeming with bird life, and on the next none is to be found, and yet to all intents and purposes both mornings are precisely alike. Again, one spell of heavy weather will drive flocks of fowl inland, while a second may have just the opposite effect, and drive them away again. The subject offers considerable food for thought, and is of great interest to the naturalist sportsman. Used as a kind of half-way house, the wide expanses of fresh water offer sanctuary to passing fowl, which gladly avail themselves of the chance to rest awhile, before proceeding to their destination, landwards or seawards. Birds, such as ducks and waders, arriving from the coast, welcome the prospect of a change of diet, such a change doubtless being of great benefit to them. There is certainly a marked difference for the better in the flavour of ducks on the table after they have spent a few days on fresh-water before being shot. I have repeatedly found that new arrivals from the sea are not very palatable, while their congeners, procured a few days later, have proved to be in fine condition, and without a trace of the marine diet upon which they had previously been subsisting. The foregoing remarks are not to be taken as implying migration lines. The flight-line described is traversed by wildfowl

WIELDING THE
CREEPING STICKS

LOADING THE
BIG GUN.

which have settled in the district at least temporarily, and in the case of some species, for the winter ; birds on migration flight pass over the district entirely, with the exception of certain summer or winter visitors, according to the season.

There is a shorter and fairly regular morning and evening flight of fowl, principally ducks, green plover, and snipe, from and to Skipwith Common, a distance of three miles only, to the usual haunt in Wheldrake Ings. To a certain extent, this flight is governed by the state of quietude pertaining to the neighbourhood.

The birds may rest in the flooded Ings all day, and fly to the Common to feed in its numerous marshy places at night, or they may elect to stay and feed in the Ings, or vice versa. Very often a number stay, and a number go away either at dawn or dusk, according as it may happen whether they are resting in the Ings and feeding at Skipwith or resting at Skipwith and feeding in the Ings. Again if shot at by the keepers on the Common, they fly across to Wheldrake, or Aughton Ings, or vice-versa. What flight-shooting is done at Cottingwith takes place on the line from Skipwith, but as it is detrimental, in fact, ruinous, to the chance of successful punt-shooting, it is looked upon disapprovingly by the old wildfowler, and he does all he can to discourage the practice. He rarely indulges in flight-shooting himself, as wild fowl must be allowed every possible opportunity to rest and regain confidence, and so enable the puntsman to approach their lynx-eyed companies. How wary ducks can be is not realised by anyone who has not attempted to shoot them. I myself have been out, and have also watched Snowden Slights spend a whole day, following companies of ducks round an area of not more than three square miles, and not once would they permit the punt to approach nearer than one hundred yards. This was the result of too open weather and of flight-shooting. However, their great reluctance to quit the edge of the ice sometimes makes it quite an easy matter to "creep" (propel the punt) within thirty yards of them, and secure a splendid shot with the big gun.

CHAPTER IV.

PUNTS AND PUNT-SHOOTING.

THE style of punt adopted by Snowden Slights is peculiar to the lower Derwent Valley; its pattern is most nearly approached by the single-handed "sneak boat" of the neighbourhood of the Wash, but, as a rule, the latter craft differs in having a coaming, and being partly decked, whereas the punt depicted in my photographs is quite open, and is generally much more frail in its construction. In appearance, the punt in question looks a most unstable creation, but in reality it is quite steady, and capable of being manœuvred with considerable ease. I think improvement might be made in the method of propulsion, but I am writing upon that relied on by the old wildfowler, and therefore perhaps ought not to digress.

A good number of gunning-punts are to be seen in the Cottingwith district, but as most of them have at one time or another been the property of Snowden Slights, and, as nearly all of them are practically of the same build, a description of the last new one and its dimensions will meet the requirements of this chapter.

The extreme length of the punt over-all is seventeen feet, the beam (width) amidships two feet ten inches, and depth from keel to edge of gunwale ten inches ; the mean draught, when loaded with the big gun and the wildfowler, being about four inches only. This is an advantage, as it enables the puntsman to follow his quarry in very shallow places. It is built of carefully selected half-inch pine, free from knots, the joints lapped over, and rivetted the whole of their length (technically known as "clinker" building)—the "strakes," or boards, being cut full length, and average about three inches in width and are "flared" up from the keel, which is cut from one piece of redwood, one inch thick, and selected without a fault, to make a flat bottom twelve inches wide amidships, and tapering evenly towards each end, where the elm bow and stern posts are screwed to it; the ribs are fixed last, and are spaced about nine inches apart. A narrow strip one inch thick is screwed along the centre of the keel, to ensure "grip" and correct steering, this latter being done during propulsion, no rudder being fitted, as it might interfere with the working of the punt rather than assisting it. A further narrow strip of wood is screwed inside the gunwale to stiffen the punt, and it is also made more rigid by a very short piece of decking, fitted fore and aft, the forward deck serving as a rest for the punt-gun. A short chain and spike are secured to an eye-bolt, and this serves both to moor the punt and to drag it out of the water and over banks when such procedure becomes necessary. The false bottom is formed in one piece, and does not extend the full length of the punt. To the forward end of this board is screwed a strong block hollowed to fit the heel of the gun-stock; the balance of the gun being found, an iron crutch is fixed in the punt at that place, so that when all is finished, the fowler, laid full-length behind the gun, is able to tilt or slightly depress the muzzle by pressure upon the stock. Horizontal motion is imparted by moving the boat, by working the propelling poles, or "creeping sticks," until the gun is brought to bear. The bottom board takes the whole impact of the recoil, and is left loose, so that it will slide in the punt something like the "bootjack" recoil apparatus, used by some coast gunners. But as this board carries the whole weight of the wildfowler, it seldom moves farther than a few inches. To propel the punt, a double paddle is used to negotiate expanses of open water where it is unnecessary to keep out of sight of wildfowl; a ten-foot "stower" (punt pole shod with an iron fork) imparts momentum when it is desired to pole along by the river banks, or proceed across places where the bottom can be readily reached. Considerable skill is required to accomplish this work, and I remember an instance of an enthusiastic sportsman attempting it. This gentleman had responded to a friendly invitation extended by Snowden Slights, to come over and try to get a shot from the punt, and was duly installed in the punt, but as he had to traverse a considerable distance before it became necessary to lie flat on the bottom on the little craft, he stood up, and boldly pushed along with the aid of the stower. Having had some experience of sea-going punts, he was rather confident, and was suddenly the recipient of a rude shock. Chancing to cross a part where the bottom was composed of rather tenacious clay, the iron grain sank deeply as the pressure was put upon it.

In the natural order of events, it should have come away easily on being pulled; the psychological moment arrived to withdraw the "stower" ready for another thrust. My sporting friend realised the pole had stuck; he felt the punt go steadily onward, and, too late, he found he should have let go the stick, and returned for it, but, unfortunately, at that moment he had passed over the end of the punt into the icy embrace of rather less than three feet of water, from which, when he had found his legs, he waded ashore, leaving the offending "stower" still sticking upright in the mud, mutely triumphant at his discomfiture.

The most important part in the propelling of the punt is that played by the "creeping sticks." These are two slender shafts, an inch thick, and from six to eight feet long, and shod with iron forks, splayed to an angle which admits of their being withdrawn from the mud without much trouble. The puntsman extended full length upon the bottom board, his face level with the trigger of the big gun, is able to take the end of one of the "creeping sticks" in each hand; the iron fork causes the opposite end to sink easily to the bottom and retain that position; I may here say that the propelling sticks must be weighted, as the prone position does not give the fowler much command of a stick that is constantly striving to float upward, rather than keep its place just trailing the bottom.

It will be readily seen that all that is then necessary is to keep drawing and thrusting evenly with both shafts, and the punt moves forward in the direction desired. Steering is done by putting more weight upon the thrust opposite the point the head of the punt is required to take, and niceties of steadiness are attained by dragging the bottom with the iron-shod sticks. The whole process appears marvellously simple, but it is quite the hardest and most back-breaking task the writer ever experienced, and it takes quite a long time to arrive at anything approaching dexterity in the business.

I must not overlook explaining that the flooded water-meadows over which this style of punting holds favour,

extend for miles with very little variation in depth ; wide
expanses often average little more than eighteen inches
in depth, and the deepest portions are seldom more than
three to four feet. Of course, I have not taken account of
the river and the numerous intersecting dykes, where the
depth increases from ten to thirty feet, but as the fowler
knows the position of the dykes, and the punt usually has
sufficient momentum to cross them, they do not occasion
much trouble.

In the unlucky event of the punt stopping over one of
these deep places, the puntsman would be obliged to get up
from his prone position to use the paddle, and would at
once scare away any ducks towards which he might have
been "setting."

Before leaving the subject of punt construction, it occurs
to me that those of my readers who are wildfowlers will
raise the question, "Why has the usual coast type of punt
been rejected in this locality?" There can be no doubt that
a double-handed, or even a single-handed sea-going punt is
a far more stable craft than the one above described ; the
extensive decking and coaming, and greater beam, make it
an eminently desirable punt for comfort, roominess, and
safety. A further advantage is the possession of a sail—a
great help when traversing distances. When "setting"
to fowl in a decked punt, the little vessel has to be propelled
by means of a short scull, working in a spur or rowlock,
fitted in the gunwale aft, and, owing to the wide beam, it
is impossible to stretch the arms far enough to operate a
pair of "creeping sticks." The shallowness of the water
prevents the use of a scull over more than two-thirds of
the punting area worked by Snowden Slights, hence the need
of a punt specially designed to meet the requirements of the

district. No doubt it could be much further improved ;
that it actually does the work required of it I hope to show
my readers in a future chapter.

The foregoing dimensions are those of the last new punt ;
two older ones measure eighteen feet long, two feet eleven
inches beam, and twelve inches deep, and sixteen feet long,
two feet ten inches beam, and eleven and a half inches deep
respectively.

Lieutenant Whitaker, late of the West Yorks. Regiment,
an enthusiastic amateur wildfowler, brought up a double-
handed punt from the Thames estuary. This was a very
useful craft in its proper place on salt water, but eventually
proved to be quite useless here, as it was utterly impossible
to work the scull when "setting" to fowl. This punt had
been made unsinkable by nailing cork on the outside of the
top strake, and, as it was roomy and steady, it ultimately
became reduced to the position of a ferry boat across the
river, first having the deck and coamings knocked out and
replaced by rude thwarts.

And now for our second subject, punt-shooting.

Many sportsmen decry punt-shooting as unsportsmanlike,
but I generally find, on questioning their attitude, that they
are quite inexperienced in this branch of sport, and in
many cases have never seen a punt-gun fired. Let me here
state that to be a successful punt-gunner, one has to possess
a knowledge of the habits of the quarry, and a skill in
approaching and shooting it, which is not required of a
sportsman in any other branch of shooting. It is essential
for the puntsman to be inured to hardship, as the pursuit
of his beloved sport is only possible under such conditions
of weather as would drive even the hardiest follower of

SNOWDEN SLIGHTS (from a photograph by Oxley Grabham).

A DERWENT VALLEY FOWLER.

field-sports home to blazing logs, in preference to continuing the quest of pheasant, hare, or partridge.

Punt-shooting in the pursuit of wild duck is a necessity, because they are unapproachable in any other manner ; duck decoys, laid out to capture hundreds of wild fowl, do not come within the scope of this book, and I leave them out of the question when I make the above statement. Wild duck and allied species of fowl frequenting wide expanses of open water are generally so shy that they rarely come within shot of the landsman's firearm. A few, certainly, are shot as they pass overhead on their regular flights, but for a professional fowler to rely upon flight-shooting for his livelihood would be akin to committing suicide. It is essential that surer means of securing the birds in paying quantities be adopted, and as the wildfowler has neither the means nor the opportunity to erect an elaborately planned decoy, he has perforce to become a punt-gunner. His sole aims are—to shoot as many duck as he possibly can with every discharge of his punt-gun, to keep down the cost of powder and lead, and to make as much profit as he can, from the result.

There is another item which he must not lose sight of, and that is—the disturbance made by the deafening report when the gun is fired. Naturally, this terrific noise puts every duck for miles on the wing, and they do not immediately settle down again after it. Also, when they have been fired at several times, they become most chary of allowing the punt to approach within range. Under such circumstances, it behoves the wildfowler to make the best of his opportunity, and shoot to kill as many birds as the gun can be aligned upon.

Most standard works on wildfowling give details anent

the best time to fire at wildfowl ; the opinion of Snowden
Slights, based upon seventy years' experience, may be worth
recording. He states that the shot he prefers with the
punt-gun is at a flock of wild duck sitting upon the ice,
and preferably at a range of thirty-five to forty yards.
Under such circumstances, they are, as a rule, packed fairly
close together, and it is possible occasionally to make sure
of the whole flock of from ten to forty individuals. The
next most successful punt shot is taken at fowl just as they
rise from the water, and at the same range. Such a shot
requires to be accurately timed as well as aimed, for unless
the fowler is very careful, he may find the lift of the boat
causes him to shoot either over or under the rising birds,
the result being a clean miss.

Distance is bad to judge over the water, and it is safest,
when shooting in daylight, to continue to approach (if the
fowl allow it) until the irises of their eyes can be clearly
distinguished. Such a distance may appear to be twenty
yards away, until it is measured, when it turns out to be
nearer thirty-five. It very often happens, when punting,
that it is possible to secure easy shots at pairs of duck,
and small lots of three to four. Slights is a firm believer
in accepting these opportunities. When the fowl are widely
scattered, it rarely happens that they will pack sufficiently
to make a good shot possible ; the odd birds keep rising
in front of the gun, until the whole of the fowl on the water
take alarm, and it is then better policy to take the first nice
batch that offers, secure the lot, and then go home until the
main body have settled down again.

CHAPTER V.

GUNS, DRESS, AND DOGS.

AS may be readily imagined, when a wildfowler has followed his sport for over seventy years, he is likely to accumulate a fair stock of lethal weapons, and this is what happened in the case of Snowden Slights. The old man dearly loves guns, and throughout his lifetime has lost no opportunity of purchasing any weapon that his limited purse would allow of. His biggest gun, used solely for punt-shooting, was built for his father by Akrill, of Beverley, and weighed 140 lbs. This huge weapon had a barrel ten feet long, and a bore of 1¼ inches, the usual charge being 4 ounces of coarse punt powder, and 18 ounces of No. 1 shot. This gun proved to be so unwieldy, particularly when it became necessary to lift it out of the punt for the purpose of dragging the punt over a bank or shoal, that it was eventually returned to its maker to have the barrel shortened to nine feet, and turned down to a weight of about 100 lbs., the charge being correspondingly reduced. The average is 2½ ounces of powder, and 16 ounces of shot. This gun is a muzzle-loader, fired by percussion, as, in fact, are all the weapons in the old fowler's armoury, with one exception. It makes a most regular pattern, considering its wide cylinder bore, and the irregularity which must result from hand-loading, and at forty yards the spread from its shot-charge is from ten to fifteen yards, and extreme range about 200 yards.

Slights has repeatedly picked up birds which have been shot dead over 100 yards away, not, of course, slain intentionally, but they were stragglers that were in the line of the party shot at, for the wildfowler prefers them to be thirty-five yards away rather than a hundred. In his armoury, there is another big muzzle-loading punt-gun, by Akrill, similar in almost every detail to the one described, but lighter by a few pounds. Owing, however, to its tendency to shoot "high" (probably a defect in the boring), it is not as reliable as his heaviest and favourite gun. The other big gun figured in the photograph is that belonging to the late Lieutenant Whitaker, and does not concern these pages.

Two more large "duck guns," as they were popularly termed, appear on the left of the illustration ; both are $1\frac{1}{8}$-inch bore, built by Akrill, and have barrels about six feet in length. Neither of these guns is so heavy as those first described, and can be fired by a strong man from the shoulder, providing some support can be obtained for the barrel to be steadied upon. They will shoot a charge of up to ten ounces of shot, but their great fault lies in the fact of their not being heavy enough for regular use in the punt, and they are much too heavy to carry about in the hope of securing a shot from the bank. Further, no matter how strong the sportsman, a few successive shots from the shoulder with one of these "toy" punt-guns would have a very demoralising effect upon his constitution.

Slights' early shooting was principally done with long-barrelled single muzzle-loaders, which averaged 14 gauge.

THE ARMOURY.

AFTER THE SHOT.

Such guns often shoot remarkably well, but even then, he would be a good sportsman of the modern school who could eclipse the feat of Snowden Slights, by shooting eighteen snipe with one charge of shot for each bird, and without a single miss. On several occasions since then, the old fowler has shot snipe according to opportunity, and made scores without a miss of eleven, twelve, and fourteen, all single shots. He fired many thousand rounds, or, should I say, charges, from a little double fourteen-gauge muzzle-loader that was his favourite weapon. He invariably carried it in the punt for use as a "cripple stopper," and so expert did he become in its employment that if it so happened that he missed stopping a bird which he had fired at, his father enquired if he were ill. From constant use this gun became very thin in the barrels, and one day on being loaned to a farmer to shoot rabbits, through an accident due to carelessness it happened that the ends of both barrels were blown away.

Slights was very distressed about this, as he thought a great deal about all his guns, and this one in particular. In fact, the remnants were in my possession for some years but recently the old fowler requested to have them returned to him, as he thought he would like to keep them in his family as a "heirloom." His armoury was of particular interest to me, and I never tired of looking over the twenty-eight old specimens of the gunmaker's art, which Slights had collected. Most of the double and single guns were of thirteen and fourteen gauge, as already stated, but as I have no exact details of all, I can only jot down a few rough notes from memory relating to some of them.

A most peculiar weapon to handle is a five-foot barrelled 10 bore "goose gun," a thick-stocked but very light

C

muzzle-loader, which kicks like a mule when fired, and which is the product of a maker named Newton, of Grantham. None of the old guns are by eminent makers like Manton or Egg, but several are from shops which had good reputations in their day. A 13 single by Brown, London ; a double 13 bore by Roberts, London ; and a double 13 bore by T. Horsley, York, are all percussion action muzzle-loading guns. One curious old blunderbuss, a short-barrelled bell-mouthed fusil, with flint lock action, has been in the Slights family for more years than can be traced, and was made by E. Baker, of London. It is a stocky little weapon, designed for coach protection, and not wildfowling, and possesses a three-edged bayonet on the top of the barrel, which is held in place by a spring ; the latter on being released throws the bayonet forward ready to repel a close attack, and one can easily imagine it altogether to be a most deadly engine in settling those little differences which cropped up from time to time along the King's highway in the good old days.

The old blunderbuss is now in the collection of the York Museum. The double 12 bore used by the old fowler during recent years, is a heavy (9 lbs.) hammer breech-loader with Damascus barrels, built by Jeffries, of Birmingham. It has proved to be a very serviceable weapon, and was a favourite gun, until weight of years, in conjunction with the weight of the gun, proved too much for his strength, and he has had to lay it aside in favour of lighter metal. I cannot trace any items except one that relates to the prices paid or received for specimens in this armoury. Nearly all were bought at sales, which occurred in the district at intervals, and none of the guns were bought new other than the two punt-guns and the modern breech-loader. I found one record

of a gun sold by Slights which reads : "1869, December.—
— Tunnard, Esq., to Snowden Slights. To 1 large boat
gun £7 5s. 0d." This account was evidently never sent
in to Mr. Tunnard, as it is not marked "Settled."

DRESS. A man who is fortunate in possessing an iron
constitution does not usually devote much attention to
niceties of detail in his clothing, and a wildfowler, above all,
must never study such matters for a moment. The mud
and wet he has to encounter soon convert all clothing into
a semblance of that worn by a vagabond. Snowden Slights,
dressed for wildfowling, generally wore a pair of old
corduroy trousers, a thick cloth waistcoat, and a heavy
corduroy coat, well furnished with huge pockets to hold
ducks, cartridges, and a miscellaneous assortment of odd-
ments. His headgear consisted of a little cap, made of
four triangles of corduroy sewn together, and this cap had
no flap, in order that there should be no obstruction in his
line of vision. His feet were encased in a pair of heavy
boots, the tongues sewn to the tops to enable him to keep
dry-shod when ankle-deep in water. He always wore thick
worsted socks (two pairs in very cold weather), well knowing that if one's feet are warm the remainder of the body
will not be uncomfortable. As far as I know, Snowden
Slights never wore an overcoat in his life. I never saw him
with one—inquiry fails to find the person who can remember
the old wildfowler appearing in such a garment. For a
short time he took kindly to a useful waterproof gabardine
shooting suit, given to him by a friend of mine, but, tiring
of this, he passed it on to his grandson, and reverted
alternately to his hard-worn corduroys and an old cloth
suit, in preference.

I well remember a bitterly cold day, on which, with

several friends, I was rabbit-shooting. All the party were
literally perishing, in spite of being muffled in great coats
and gloves. There stood Slights, in his usual shooting
attire, and without gloves, and as we waited for the bunnies
to bolt from the ferrets, which the keepers had introduced
into their burrows, he turned to a pair of us standing near,
and said, "I think it's a little bit cold to-day, gentlemen,
there's a sharpish wind. I might have brought a pair of
old gloves, if I'd thought aught about it." My own desire
at the moment was for half a dozen extra overcoats, as
well as gloves.

Dogs. With wildfowlers the subject of dogs is always
a vexed question, and it is well I have merely in this
direction to recount the tastes of one individual. A good
dog is a vital necessity to a wildfowler, and Slights invariably pinned his faith to the retriever. For punt-shooting
he thought a spaniel very useful, but generally a spaniel
proves to be not strong enough to keep going through a
hard day's work. Compared with the retriever, the spaniel
is the more restless of the two, and a more difficult subject
to break into punt-work. To be a punt-shooter's dog, the
animal must be quiet of tongue, of body, and absolutely
without a trace of gun-shyness. It must retrieve any kind
of fur and feather, the latter invariably through water
and lastly, it must retrieve quickly to hand without any fuss

My shooting readers will readily understand the difficulty
of breaking a retriever to lie perfectly still, with head flat
and body extended, under the barrel of a punt-gun, sometimes for hours at a stretch, and then never to flinch when
the big gun was fired. The old wildfowler could not
accustom a spaniel faithfully to perform all these foregoing
duties, but found a small retriever, either flat or curly-

SLIGHTS WITH
STANLEY
DUNCAN,
PUTTING
GUN INTO PUNT.

SNOWDEN SLIGHTS' GREAT-GRANDSON WITH HIS ARMOURY.

coated, to be the most tractable. He considered the curly variety to be the most hardy. His last canine friend— a small but strong wavy-coated retriever—was a most sagacious brute. Poor old "Ben" would lie under the big gun and not move a muscle at the discharge, and on being ordered to fetch a bird, he would slip over the edge of the punt as carefully as his owner might have done. Not long ago the old dog, during a protracted illness of his master, was sent to me for a time, and we became great friends. But another shooting season came round, and he returned home to his duties. Wandering away from his kennel one day, he never returned. Whether someone shot or poisoned the old fellow I know not, but I have a shrewd suspicion he WAS shot, which was a great pity. He has not been replaced, nor is likely to be, as Slights, at his advanced age, would hardly be equal to the labour of training another dog to the same pitch of perfection. I miss old "Ben" much, and regret I did not make some proposal to Slights to keep him altogether.

When looking over some old papers I found a dog licence issued in 1870 to John Slights. It is a curiosity when compared with the licence of to-day. It is also cheaper, and reads :—

LICENCE TO KEEP ONE DOG ONLY,
to 31st December, 1870.

No. C 60806.   York Collection District.

I, being duly authorised by the Commissioners of Inland Revenue, do here by licence John Slights, residing at East Cottingwith, in the Parish of East Cottingwith and County of York, to keep one dog from the date hereof until the 31st day of December,

1870, he having paid the sum of Five Shillings for this Licence. Dated this 29th day of January, 1870.
(Signed)   WM. CORBETT.

On the reverse side is printed :—

This Licence should be renewed in January every year. The penalty for keeping a dog above six months old without a licence is Five Pounds.

CHAPTER VI.

The Birds of the Derwent Valley.

I N devoting this chapter to the birds of the Derwent Valley a full list of birds, the one hundred and twenty-seven that occur, or are known to have occurred, in the particular area which concerns this book, is given. I wish it to be distinctly understood that this list, however, is not intended to cover the full length of the course of the river, but that portion only which is described in Chapter III. All species that are not wildfowl are very briefly dealt with, as they are only included to enable a naturalist to turn to these pages for reference, should he so choose to honour me. In the case of rare and uncommon species, the actual records are given as far as it is possible, and, where actual dates are omitted, very careful inquiry has been made before the inclusion of a species.

Each species is described according to its being either resident, common, occasional, or rare summer or winter visitor. The description of form and colour of the birds has not been attempted, as such a proceeding would be superfluous, in view of the large number of present-day works dealing with our British birds, to which an interested student usually has easy access. Local names are always

39

of interest, and one (or more) has been included with each species that is dubbed with such distinctive appellations.

MISSEL THRUSH (Turdus viscivorus).—Common resident.

SONG THRUSH (Turdus musicus).—Common resident.

REDWING (Turdus iliacus).—Common winter visitor, arrives during September and October.

FIELDFARE (Turdus pilaris).—Common winter visitor, arrives during September and October.

BLACKBIRD (Turdus merula).—Common resident.

WHEATEAR (Saxicola œnanthe).—Occasional spring visitor, arrives middle of March.

WHINCHAT (Pratincola rubetra).—Summer visitor, arrives first week in May.

REDSTART (Ruticilla phœnicurus).—Summer visitor, arrives middle of April.

REDBREAST (Erithacus rubecula).—Common resident.

NIGHTINGALE (Daulias luscinia).—Occasional summer visitor, and heard in May.

WHITETHROAT (Sylvia rufa).—Common summer visitor, arrives early in April.

LESSER WHITETHROAT (Sylvia curruca).—Summer visitor, arrives end of April.

BLACKCAP (Sylvia atricapilla).—Summer visitor, arrives end of April.

GARDEN WARBLER (Sylvia salicaria).—Summer visitor, arrives first week in May.

GOLDEN-CRESTED WREN (Regulus cristatus).—Rare as a breeding species, but very common in the woods during November ; most of them winter immigrants from the Continent.

CHIFF-CHAFF (Phylloscopus collybita).—Common summer visitor, arrives end of March.

WILLOW-WARBLER (Phylloscopus trochilus).—Common summer visitor, arrives first week in April.

WOOD-WARBLER (Phylloscopus sibilatrix).—Summer visitor, comparatively rare, arrives early in May.

SEDGE-WARBLER (Acrocephalus phragmitis).—Summer visitor ; arrives last week in April.

GRASSHOPPER-WARBLER (Locustella naevia).—Rare summer visitor, arrives first week in May.

HEDGE ACCENTOR (Accentor modularis).—Local name "Cuddy," common resident.

DIPPER OR WATER OUSEL (Cinclus aquaticus).—Resident in Yorkshire, but a rare visitor to this locality ; one was shot by Slights on October 7th, 1867. It is sometimes seen at Sutton dam.

LONG-TAILED TIT (Acredula caudata).—Local name "Bottle tit." Rare in summer. Sometimes occurs in good numbers about November ; no doubt they are foreign immigrants.

GREAT TIT (Parus major).—Local name "Billy-biter." Resident, but not common.

COAL TIT (Parus ater).—Local name "Blackcap." Resident, but not common.

MARSH TIT (Parus palustris).—Local name "Blackcap." Resident, but not common.

BLUE TIT (Parus caeruleus).—Local name "Blue cap," "Tom-tit," and "Billy-biter." Common resident.

CREEPER (Certhia familiaris).—Resident, but rare ; there is a slight increase in winter.

COMMON WREN (Troglodytes parvulus).—Common resident.

PIED WAGTAIL (Motacilla lugubris).—Local name "Peggy Wagtail. " Resident.

GREY WAGTAIL (Motacilla melanope).—Resident in Yorkshire, but rare in this locality.

YELLOW OR RAYS WAGTAIL (Motacilla raii).—Summer visitor ; arrives in mid-April.

TREE PIPIT (Anthus trivialis).—Summer visitor ; arrives about middle of April.

MEADOW PIPIT (Anthus pratensis).—Local name "Titlark." Resident ; there is also a fairly large influx in April.

GREAT GREY SHRIKE (Lanius excubitor).—Local name "Butcher bird." Winter visitor. Has several times been shot by Slights. There is a stuffed specimen at East Cottingwith without data.

SPOTTED FLYCATCHER (Musicapa grisola).—Common summer visitor ; arrives early in May.

SWALLOW (Hirundo rustica).—Common summer visitor ; arrives first week in April. Several white varieties have occurred.

HOUSE MARTIN (Chelidon urbica).—Common summer visitor; arrives second week in April. A beautiful white variety was shot at Escrick during August, 1895.

SAND MARTIN (Cotile riparia).—Common summer visitor ; arrives early in April.

GOLDFINCH (Carduelis elegans).—Resident. The numbers are augmented in winter.

SISKIN (Chrysomitris spinus).—Occasional winter visitor.

GREENFINCH (Ligurinus chloris).—Very common resident.

HAWFINCH (Coccothraustes vulgaris).—Resident ; but not common.

HOUSE SPARROW (Passer domesticus).—Very common resident.

TREE SPARROW (Passer montanus).—Common resident.

CHAFFINCH (Fringilla cœlebs).—Common resident.

BRAMBLING (Fringilla montifringilla).—Winter visitor, but erratic ; sometimes occurs in large flocks.

MEALY REDPOLL (Linota linaria).—Rare ; winter visitor.

LESSER REDPOLL (Linota rufescens).—Resident, but uncommon ; the numbers are augmented in winter.

LINNET (Linota cannabina).—Common resident.

TWITE (Linota flavirostris).—Occasional visitor ; has bred at Skipwith.

BULLFINCH (Pyrrhula europæa).—Resident ; numbers are annually decreasing.

CROSSBILL (Loxia curvirostra).—Occasional winter visitor.

COMMON BUNTING (Emberiza miliaria).—Local names "Corn Bunting" and "Big Bunting." Resident, but not common.

YELLOW BUNTING (Emberiza citrinella).—Common resident. Local name "Yellow Ammer."

REED BUNTING (Emberiza schnœniclus).—Resident ; the bulk of this species migrate in winter. Numbers of immatures are caught by bird-catchers in the autumn, and are generally dubbed "squeakers" by these men.

SNOW BUNTING (Plectrophanes nivalis).—Very rare winter visitor. One was shot by Snowden Slights on Jan. 24th, 1868.

SKYLARK (Alauda arvensis).—Common resident ; more numerous in winter than summer.

STARLING (Sturnus vulgaris).—Very common resident. Local name "Gippy," and "Gip" starling.

MAGPIE (Pica rustica).—Residents ; gamekeepers take care they do not become common.

ROOK (Corvus frugilegus).—Common resident. There are several large colonies.

CARRION CROW (Corvus corone).—Resident. Gamekeepers keep the number within limits.

HOODED CROW (Corvus cornix).—Common winter visitor. Local name "Greyback."

SWIFT (Cypselus apus).—Common summer visitor ; arrives first week in May.

NIGHTJAR (Caprimulgus europæus).—Summer visitor ; about ten pairs usually nest at Skipwith; arrives early in May.

GREAT SPOTTED WOODPECKER (Picus major).—Resident ; numbers appear to be slightly increasing.

GREEN WOODPECKER (Gecinus viridis).—Resident ; numbers appear to be slightly increasing.

KINGFISHER (Alcedo ispida).—Resident ; not common, but now slightly increasing.

CUCKOO (Cuculus canorus).—Summer visitor. Arrives second week in April.

BARN OWL (Strix flammea).—Resident. Thanks to better protection now afforded these species, they are becoming rather more common.

SHORT-EARED OWL (Asio accipitrinus).—Winter visitor ; occurs during October and November.

LITTLE OWL (Athene noctua).—Very rare ; there is a record of one having occurred at Escrick in 1896.

MONTAGUS HARRIER (Circus cineraceus).—Very rare. Mr. Nelson states that it has occurred at Skipwith. ("Birds of Yorkshire," page 323.)

GOSHAWK (Astur palumbarius).—Very rare. Mr. W. Hewett, of York, records the capture of one at Escrick in 1896. (See "Birds of Yorkshire," p. 341).

SPARROW HAWK (Accipter nisus).—Resident. Is prevented from becoming common by the gamekeepers.

KESTREL (Falco tennunculus).—Resident. Is prevented from

POLING THE
PUNT.

SEDGE WARBLER AND YOUNG.

becoming common by the gamekeepers. Numbers are augmented by immigrants during the autumn.

It is possible that more of the rarer hawks have occurred in this district, as Snowden Slights' book contains numerous records of hawks obtained by him, but unfortunately no attempt has been made to distinguish between different species, and it is unlikely they were all of the same species.

CORMORANT (Phalacrocorax carbo).—Occasional visitor. One was shot on April 13th, 1872.

GANNET (Sula bassana).—Occasional visitor. They are usually immature birds, with black and white spreckled plumage, and those obtained have sometimes been mistaken for specimens of the Great Northern Diver, which does not occur here.

HERON (Ardea cinerea).—Resident. More numerous in winter. The bulk of the birds probably come from the heronry at Moreby, which is adjacent.

BITTERN (Botaurus stellaris).—Rare winter visitor. One shot at East Cottingwith on December 16th, 1867, another at the same place on December 6th, 1868, and the last was obtained in Wheldrake Ings, January 18th, 1905; this bird was 27 inches high, 28 inches from tip of beak to tail, and was 44 inches across the expanded wings. It was a beautiful male example, and is now in my collection.

SPOONBILL (Platalea leucorodia).—Very rare visitor. Slights states that he has shot two specimens, but cannot trace any notes concerning them. According to "Birds of Yorkshire," the late Sir William Milner had one in his collection, which had been obtained from Wilberfoss, August 2nd, 1851.

WHITE-FRONTED GOOSE (Anser albifrons).—Winter visitor. This is the bird generally described as "goose" in Slights' records, the particular species not being distinguished ; they occur every winter. A definite instance is, two were shot on January 2nd, 1904, but as they are not rare, there is no need to publish further dates.

PINK-FOOTED GOOSE (Anser brachyrhynchus).—Winter visitor, also described by Slights as "goose" only. It occurs in small flocks nearly every winter. One shot at East Cottingwith, January 5th, 1906, is now in the York Museum.

BEAN GOOSE (Anser segetum).—Occasional winter visitor. The foregoing remarks also apply to this species, but it is much rarer. One was shot at East Cottingwith in January, 1903, and is described in "Birds of Yorkshire." I have records of others that have been shot by Snowden Slights during recent years.

BRENT GOOSE (Bernicla brenta).—Occasional winter visitor. This species prefers salt water, and does not often favour the Derwent Valley. They have been obtained at East Cottingwith on various occasions, the only definite dates I have are October 22nd, 1863, February 12th, 1864, and one on December 5th, 1903 ; the latter is now in my collection.

BERNACLE GOOSE (Anser leucopsis).—Rare winter visitor. Specimens have been shot by the old wildfowler several times, but there is no exact record.

WHOOPER SWAN (Cygnus musicus).—Winter visitor. The number varies according to the severity of the weather. Snowden Slights has obtained a great many at East Cottingwith, and I quote but a few dates, although I could give a long list : February 2nd, 1861 (1), February 25th (2), December 20th (2), December 23rd (2), all 1871 ; January 16th (2) and 23rd (2), February 3rd, 1875 (2), January 29th, 1876 (1). I saw two in Wheldrake Ings in November, 1910, and shot one of them.

BEWICK'S SWAN (Cygnus Bewickii).—Rare visitor. Has been obtained at East Cottingwith several times, but the actual dates cannot be traced. One specimen came into my possession that had been shot in Wheldrake Ings on March 2nd, 1903.

MUTE SWAN (Cygnus olor).—This is the domesticated species, and, although a number have been obtained in the Derwent Valley, I am of the opinion that they have all been birds which have strayed from private ownership.

BLACK SWAN (Cygnus nigricollis).—One, probably an escape, was shot by Snowden Slights about fifteen years ago.

SHELDRAKE (Tadorna cornuta).—Occasional visitor. This species prefers the neighbourhood of the sea, and does not often appear so far inland as East Cottingwith. One was shot on January 11th, 1876, five on January 13th, 1883, and one on January 23rd, 1904. This latter bird is now in my collection.

WILD DUCK OR MALLARD (Anas boscas).—Resident, and by far the most common species of wildfowl found in the Derwent Valley. Details regarding the vast number shot by Snowden Slights will be found under "Details of Punt-gun Shots." Varieties have sometimes occurred, but actual records are difficult to trace. A beautiful white drake was shot on April 6th, 1870, and a hybrid between the pintail and mallard was

obtained by Slights during the 'eighties. The present
whereabouts of this variety is unfortunately unknown.
A partial albino, and also a mallard that possesses a
slate-coloured, instead of green head, both obtained
in the Derwent Valley, are in the writer's collection.
An exceedingly dark variety that had been shot at
East Cottingwith was exhibited before the York
Field Naturalists' Society on December 9th, 1885, by
Mr. James Backhouse, jun.

GADWALL (Anas strepera).—Rare winter visitor. Several
have been shot by Snowden Slights, but of these only
two notes can be traced, one bird being obtained at
East Cottingwith, December 18th, 1867, and another
on January 29th, 1869. Mr. Nelson, in "Birds of
Yorkshire," records one shot at East Cottingwith in
February, 1892; this is now in the York Museum.

SHOVELLER (Anas clypeata).—Resident. Breeds regularly
on Skipwith Common, and as recently at 1911 five or
six pairs nested there. They occur on the flooded
Ings every winter, but except as specimens they are
not worth powder and shot.

The following table will show at a glance the
respective dates on which certain of these birds were
shot :—

YEAR.	MONTH.	NO. OF BIRDS SHOT.
1872	October 5th.	7
1872	,, 7th.	2
1874	March 4th.	2
1876	October 25th.	3
1881	September 10th.	4
1881	October 8th.	6
1881	November 19th.	1
1882	February 11th.	4

Their local name is "Spoonbill."

CRIPPLE CHASE.

SLIGHTS WITH DOG AND PUNT.

PINTAIL (Anas acuta).—Winter visitor, but rare inland. They appear in the Derwent Valley during hard weather; they have been shot at East Cottingwith as follows : (1) December 12th, 1874, (2) January 24th, (2) January 29th, 1876, (1) September 22nd, (2) September 29th, 1877, (1) on December 4th, 1885, (2) on October 23rd, 1896, and (1) on January 2nd, 1904. Local names are "Sea pheasant" and "Longtail duck."

TEAL (Anas crecca).—Resident. Breeds regularly at Skipwith. The numbers are greatly augmented in the winter, and as a rule they figure in about the same proportion as widgeon and pochard. They are locally termed "half duck." The largest number I have seen in a flock or "spring" is sixty.

GARGANEY (Anas querquedula).—Very rare winter visitor. I have no record concerning this species, but there is a specimen in Captain Dunnington-Jefferson's collection at Thicket Priory that was shot in Wheldrake Ings.

WIDGEON (Anas penelope).—Common winter visitor. Occasionally there are vast numbers of widgeon in the Derwent Valley, and particularly during continued rough weather on the coast. According to "Birds of Yorkshire" (page 460), a nest of widgeon containing twelve eggs, was discovered on Skipwith Common, May 1st, 1897. I have reason to believe this species has bred there since this date, but could not locate the nest, although I had the birds under observation for a considerable time.

POCHARD (Fuligula ferina).—Regular winter visitor. Although this species nests at Hornsea, I cannot trace it as a breeding resident at Skipwith, a very suitable

D

locality.   Snowden Slights has shot numbers at East
Cottingwith, and they are generally described in his
books as "Pokkers" and "Dunpokkers."

SCAUP (Fuligula marila).—Winter visitor.   As the scaup
prefers the sea, it does not regularly visit the Derwent
Valley.   A few have been shot almost every winter ;
a large number occurred and a quantity were shot on
January 23rd, 1904.   Local name, "Black Pokker."

TUFTED DUCK (Fuligula cristata).—Winter visitor.   I have
often watched them through a field-glass at East
Cottingwith, but have no records of specimens shot.

GOLDENEYE (Fuligula clangula).—Regular winter visitor.
Specimens have been shot at East Cottingwith on
February 4th, 1865, March 2nd and 18th, 1865.
(2) December 11th, 1865, (1) December 3rd, and (1)
December 16th, 1866, (1) February 15th, 1869, (1)
January 26th, 1870, (1) January 5th, (1) January 14th,
(1) January 21st, 1871, and (1) November 29th, 1876.

LONG-TAILED DUCK (Fuligula glacialis).—Very rare winter
visitor.   I cannot trace a definite record of this
species, but I see no reason to doubt Slights' verbal
statement that he has obtained several specimens.
On this authority Mr. Nelson includes it in his
monograph, "Birds of Yorkshire."

COMMON SCOTER (Œdemia nigra).—Occasional winter visitor.   This sea-loving species has been shot at East
Cottingwith (2) on October 23rd, 1862, (1) November
2nd, 1864, and (3) on March 6th, 1872.   Local name,
"Scotter."

HARLEQUIN DUCK (Fuligula histrionica).—Snowden Slights
informs me that in April, 1860, he shot a male and
female out of a little party of three in Wheldrake

Ings. These two rare ducks, he states, were forwarded to the Hull Museum. I have inquired from the Curator, Mr. Thos. Sheppard, as to whether the specimens are still in the collection, but no trace of them can be discovered. A few days after procuring these birds, the old fowler saw another pair in the vicinity of Ellerton, and after stalking them for some time, he obtained a shot that killed the duck but missed the drake. He sent this harlequin to York, putting a reserve sale price of five shillings upon it, and in the event of its not being sold, it was to be forwarded to Osgodby Hall. As it did not find a purchaser the instructions were carried out, and the bird was ultimately placed in the Osgodby collection, where it stayed until a few years ago, when, along with many more objects, it came under the auctioneer's hammer. Slights goes on to say that the auctioneer stated the specimen—he (the auctioneer) did not know its name—was extinct in England, and evidently worked up some competition for the prize, as it was eventually knocked down at five pounds, but as to whom the purchaser was there is no information.

GOOSANDER (Mergus merganser).—Winter visitor. As a rule, they are nearly all immature birds, and females; the proportion of adult males is very small. I have a great many records of specimens obtained at East Cottingwith : (3) January 14th, 1864, (2) February 18th, 1865, (1) January 13th, 1868, (1) November 13th, 1869, (3) November 5th, 1870, (4) December 4th, 1870, (1) January 28th, 1871, (1) November 15th, 1873, (3) December 4th, 1875 ; (1) January 11th, (1) January 13th, (1) December 27th, and (1) Decem-

ber 30th, 1876 ; (1) November 17th, 1877, (2) January
2nd, 1878, (1) March 15th and (1) December 27th,
1879 : (1) November 18th, 1880, (1) February 26th,
1881, (2) November 17th, 1883, (2) December 3rd,
1884 ; (1) February 25th, (1) December 2nd, and (2)
December 22nd, 1885. One male and three females
were shot between February 4th and 7th, 1903, and
two females on January 24th, 1907. Local name,
"Sawbill."

RED-BREASTED MERGANSER (Mergus serrator).—Rare winter
visitor. Slights states that he has shot several of
these birds, but records cannot be traced. I have a
note of a male being shot higher up the Derwent
at Kirkham Abbey on January 2nd, 1904.

SMEW (Mergus albellus).—Occasional visitor. Specimens
have been procured at East Cottingwith as follows :
(1) February 12th, 1859 ; (3) December 6th, (2) December 8th, and (1) February 20th, 1860 ; (1) February
28th, 1861, (1) February 13th, 1862, (1) December
31st, 1864, (1) January 27th, 1868, (1) December 11th,
1902. A great many immature birds are obtained,
and are not readily identified except by a naturalist.

HOODED MERGANSER (Mergus cucculatus).—Accidental
visitor. There is a beautiful adult male in Captain
Dunnington-Jefferson's collection at Thicket Priory
that was shot many years ago in Wheldrake Ings by
Snowden Slights. There is no actual record of the
the date, but the old wildfowler distinctly recollects
procuring this rare species. The bird is described in
"Birds of Yorkshire," page 486.

RINGDOVE OR WOOD-PIGEON (Columba palumbus).—Common
resident. The flocks are augmented in the autumn by

SNOWDEN
PLAXTON (right)
AND FRIEND.

AFTER A SHOT AT
GREEN PLOVER.

Continental immigrants, sometimes in immense numbers. They are very fond of resorting to the exposed banks of the flooded Ings, and thus affording opportunities to the wildfowler of securing a shot with the punt-gun ; this is why this apparently unusual bird for a wildfowler to secure, figures in the lists kept by Snowden Slights. Local name, "Stoggie."

STOCKDOVE (Columba œnas).—Resident, but rare. This species is almost ousted from the district by its stronger relative, and of late years has become comparatively scarce. A few pairs breed every year in the Thorganby coverts. Local name, "Stoggie."

TURTLE DOVE (Turtur communis).—Summer visitor. About six to twelve pairs annually nest in the Thorganby coverts, where they usually arrive the last week in April.

BLACK GROUSE (Tetrao tetrix).—Introduced. Efforts are being made to introduce this magnificent game bird on Skipwith Common by Mr. J. Morris, gamekeeper to Lord Wenlock, but up to the time of writing with but little success, foxes having accounted for those not otherwise despatched by rain and cold. I understand that Mr. Morris has not yet accepted defeat, and intends to continue his efforts during the spring of 1912.

RED GROUSE (Lagopus scoticus).—Introduced. The remarks on the black grouse equally apply to this species.

PHEASANT (Phasiana torquatus).—This popular game bird is extensively hand-reared in the district. Some beautiful white varieties occasionally occur.

PARTRIDGE (Perdix cinerea).—Resident. The district is exceptionally favourable to this bird, and during the shooting season as many as two hundred have been sent over the guns in one beat.

RED-LEGGED PARTRIDGE (Caccabis rufa).—Resident. The species is not common, probably because it is not encouraged by the proprietors of the various shootings; its well-known habit of running instead of taking to wing causes it to be out of favour as a sporting bird. As driving becomes more resorted to, the bird may come into favour, offering as it does a fine sporting shot, once it gets fairly into flight.

LANDRAIL OR CORNCRAKE (Crex pratensis).—Summer visitor. Generally arrives first week in May, and is fairly numerous. Local names, "Meadow Drake" and "Corn Drake."

SPOTTED CRAKE (Porzana maruetta).—Rare visitor. One was shot at East Cottingwith by Snowden Slights on October 31st, 1874.

WATER RAIL (Rallus aquaticus).—Resident. A few pairs regularly frequent the district. I have shot them on several occasions during the winter months, and saw two as recently as December, 1911. The nest is very difficult to discover, and I have only once succeeded in finding it.

MOORHEN OR WATERHEN (Gallinula chloropus).—Common resident. Varieties of this species are very rare, but a good light buff example is in the Thicket Priory collection, which was obtained at East Cottingwith.

COOT (Fulica atra).—Resident. Generally more common in winter. Local name, "Bald-coot."

STONE CURLEW OR NORFOLK PLOVER (Œdicnemus scolopax).—Rare visitor. Only one local occurrence is recorded when a specimen of this bird was seen near Thicket

Priory by Capt. Dunnington-Jefferson on December 24th, 1888, and noted in "Birds of Yorkshire," p. 564.

CREAM-COLOURED COURSER (Cursorius gallicus).—Accidental visitor. A single specimen was obtained about 1860 by Snowden Slights at East Cottingwith, and was sent to a Mr. Reed, of Selby, but the old wildfowler cannot supply me with more definite notes anent this rare species.

GOLDEN PLOVER (Charadrius pluvialis).—Regular winter visitor, sometimes arrives in large flocks in company with lapwings.

GREY PLOVER (Squatarola helvetica).—Winter visitor. This bird prefers salt to fresh water, and seldom occurs in larger parties than from six to twelve ; it has often been shot at East Cottingwith. I have a note of five being shot on September 17th, 1866.

RINGED PLOVER (Aegialitis hiaticula).—Winter visitor. Arrives in company with knots and golden plover, and has often been obtained.

DOTTERILL (Eudromias morinellus).—Rare winter visitor. The only note I have of the occurrence of this species at East Cottingwith is of one shot by Snowden Slights on February 25th, 1861.

LAPWING (Vanellus vulgaris).—Common resident. Occurs during the winter in vast numbers. Local names : "Peewit," "Green Plover," and "Teerfit."

OYSTER-CATCHER (Hæmatopus ostralegus).—Accidental visitor. Slights states that he has shot several examples, but has no definite record.

AVOCET (Recurvirostris avocetta).—Accidental visitor. According to "Birds of Yorkshire," two were seen on Skipwith Common about 1880.

BLACK-WINGED STILT (**Himantopus** candidus).—Accidental visitor. 1 am able to add five new records of this species to the Yorkshire list ; one was shot at East Cottingwith by Snowden Slights on April 2nd, 1860, two on September 30th, 1860—evidently a pair—and on October 2nd, 1860, the old wildfowler obtained another pair. Apparently the year 1860 was marked by a small visitation of this interesting species, which Slights refers to as "Long-legs" and "Stilt Plover." The stilt has not again occurred since 1860.

WOODCOCK (Scolopax rusticula).—Resident. Is more numerous in winter.

GREAT SNIPE (Gallinago major).—Occasional visitor. Has several times been shot by Snowden Slights at East Cottingwith.

COMMON SNIPE (Gallinago cœlestis).—Resident. Large numbers arrive in winter.

JACK SNIPE (Gallinago gallinula).—Winter visitor. Sometimes very numerous. Local name; "Judcock."

DUNLIN (Tringa alpina).—Winter visitor. Has been shot at East Cottingwith many times, occasionally in large numbers with the punt-gun.

KNOT (Tringa canutus).—Winter visitor. Usually prefers salt to fresh water, but has been obtained at East Cottingwith as follows : (2) October 1st, 1860, (1) March 2nd, 1862, (8) March 18th, 1865, (3) October 21st, 1871, (4) September 6th, 1881. I saw a flock of nine early in December, 1911, but did not shoot at them.

SANDERLING (Calidris arenaria).—Winter visitor. Local name, "Stint." Has often been obtained.

RUFF (Machetes pugnax).—Spring and autumn visitor. There are several examples in the Thicket Priory collection, which have been obtained locally, and a note in my possession of a reeve shot on March 29th, 1859, probably refers to one of them.

COMMON SANDPIPER (Totanus hypoleucus).—Spring visitor. Is often seen on passage, but does not stop to nest in the district.

REDSHANK (Totanus calidris).—Resident. Breeds on the "Ings" in good numbers.

SPOTTED REDSHANK (Totanus fuscus).—Accidental visitor. One was shot at East Cottingwith in August, 1896 ("Birds of Yorkshire," page 636). This bird is now in the York Museum.

GREENSHANK (Totanus canescens).—Rare winter visitor. I have a note of one shot at East Cottingwith on September 10th, 1881. It rarely comes so far inland.

BAR-TAILED GODWIT (Limosa aegocephala).—Rare winter visitor. One was procured at East Cottingwith by Snowden Slights on November 18th, 1876.

CURLEW (Numenius arquata).—Resident. They occasionally nest on Skipwith Common, but usually only an odd pair. A few occur as immigrants during the winter, and several are generally obtained. Records of their nesting are detailed on page 645 of "Birds of Yorkshire."

WHIMBREL (Numenius phæpus).—Spring visitor. A good many were shot by Snowden Slights before the passing of the Wild Birds' Protection Acts, and were generally obtained during May; hence their local name of "May bird." They were also called "Jack Curlews."

BLACK TERN (Hydrochelidon nigra).—Spring visitor. Often occurs on Skipwith Common during May.

COMMON TERN (Sterna fluviatilis).—Rare visitor. One was shot by Snowden Slights on September 10th, 1881, at East Cottingwith. Local name, "Sea swallow."

LITTLE GULL (Larus minutus).—Rare winter visitor. According to "Birds of Yorkshire," two were shot on Skipwith Common, September 1st, 1856.

BLACK-HEADED GULL (Larus ridibundus).—Resident. There is a large breeding colony on Skipwith Common ; the numbers have increased lately during late years. I estimated that there were between 800 and 1,000 pairs nesting in June, 1911.

COMMON GULL (Larus canus).—Winter visitor. Small parties visit the flooded "Ings" practically every winter.

HERRING GULL (Larus argentatus).—Fairly common winter visitor.

LESSER BLACK-BACKED GULL (Larus fuscus).—Occasional winter visitor.

GREAT BLACK-BACKED GULL (Larus marinus).—Rare winter visitor. One was shot at East Cottingwith, February 15th, 1869.

KITTIWAKE (Rissa tridactyla).—Winter visitor. Small flocks of these gulls have frequently been mistaken for duck in the bad light of nightfall, when Slights has erased such parties with the deadly discharge of his punt-gun.

POMATORHINE SKUA (Stercorarius pomatorhinus).—Rare visitor. One was found dead on Skipwith Common in October, 1858. "Birds of Yorkshire," page 701.

BLACK-THROATED DIVER (Colymbus arcticus).—Accidental winter visitor. One was obtained at East Cottingwith on October 30th, 1875, one on January 11th, 1876, and another on November 19th, 1881.

RED-THROATED DIVER (Colymbus septentrionalis).—Occasional winter visitor. Two were shot at East Cottingwith by Snowden Slights on November 27th, 1875. One on January 18th, 1876, and an immature bird on December 20th, 1895. This latter is now in the York Museum.

GREAT CRESTED GREBE (Lophæthyia cristata).—Winter visitor. Specimens have been obtained at East Cottingwith on November 18th, 1876 ; January 21st, 1885 ; November 6th, 1885 ; February 17th, 1897, and a male in breeding plumage was shot there on June 19th, 1905, and was in my collection previously to being placed in the York Museum. One was also obtained on January 5th, 1910.

SCLAVONIAN GREBE (Dytes auritus).—Rare winter visitor. One was shot at East Cottingwith on December 3rd, and another on December 16th, 1898. Another one was obtained at East Cottingwith on February 10th, 1912. Local name, "Horned Grebe."

EARED GREBE (Podiceps nigricollis).—Accidental visitor. There is a single specimen in Captain Dunnington-Jefferson's collection at Thicket Priory which is believed to have been shot by Snowden Slights.

LITTLE GREBE (Podiceps fluviatilis).—Resident. Generally more common in winter ; several may often be seen disporting together in the river Derwent. Local name, "Puffin" and "Tom Pudding" ; also "Little Diver."

CHAPTER VII.

WILDFOWL AND WILDFOWLING.

THE question is sometimes asked, "What birds can be justly included in the category of wildfowl?" Well, the reader will find I have gone into this matter in a future chapter (chapter xi.), where he will find certain statistical details. However, I will assume for the purposes of this chapter that mallard or wild duck, widgeon, teal, pochard and green plover constitute the principal species classed as wildfowl. Other species that are worthy of powder and shot, but which do not figure conspicuously on the list, are pintail, swan, goose, golden plover and snipe. The reason the numbers are comparatively small in the chapter alluded to, is that the list is made up from "punt-gun shots"; it takes no account of bags made with the shoulder gun. Where species like snipe are included, as the result of big gun shooting, it does not necessarily follow that the shot taken was at such small fry; rather does it point to the fact that certain snipe happened to be in "good company," and thus were gathered in along with nobler quarry.

In the Derwent Valley, wildfowl such as pintail, shoveller, and tufted duck, swans, and geese, are seldom found in

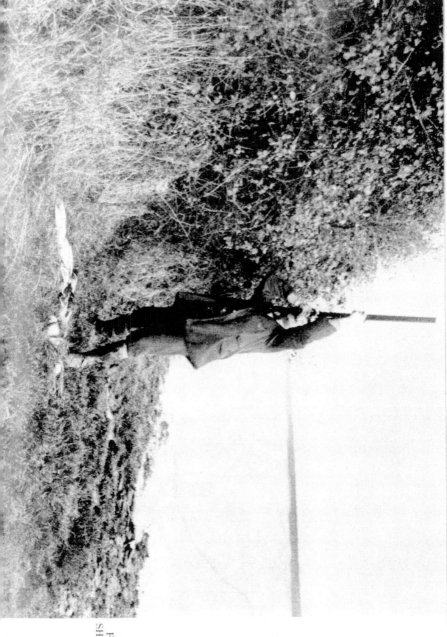

FLIGHT SHOOTING.

GROUP OF
HARVEST
SHOOTERS.

large numbers, and often enough the old wildfowler would
not loose off the big gun to secure even a party of six
or more, when by a little careful management he could
manœuvre them close together, and secure the lot at one
shot from his "cripple stopper."

As no record whatever has been kept of shoulder gun
shots, or punt-gun shots, previous to 1890, details are not
forthcoming of the vast numbers of wildfowl procured by
Snowden Slights, and his father before him, which par-
ticulars would have been of great interest to present-day
sportsmen.

The old wildfowler looked upon everything endowed with
feathers on—other than pheasants and partridges (these he
most religiously regarded as not for him)—as legitimate prey
and he followed out his motto, "Shoot first and ask
questions afterwards," to the very letter. Whether or not
he was justified, I am not prepared to say, but he found a
market for all and sundry, and, according to his old account
books, a bundle of wretched starlings fetched their price as
readily as a couple of "heavy" duck. No doubt some unfortunate purchaser duly regretted the deal, but as long as
starlings "went off" in the market, just as surely did the
big gun "go off" whenever it was in the way of a congre-
gation (flock). Towards the end of September and the early
part of October, large flocks of green plover or lapwings
would spread themselves over the "Ings." As a rule, there
would not be much water out there at this time of the year,
and the scarcer the water, the scarcer the plover. These
creatures love to frequent the vicinity of wide-spreading
shallows, and if there is plenty of adjacent fallow land, then
so much the better, as in the latter case a plentiful supply
of food is assured.

Under such conditions they will fly at regular intervals between the water and the uplands, and thus offer good flight-shooting, and when at rest on the exposed shoals and mud-banks, they furnish excellent chances to the fowler of securing a shot at them with his punt-gun. How effective is this method may be judged from an instance where Slights fired at seventy-six green plover resting upon a bank, and with but one exception secured the lot. During the hours of daylight, wild duck of all sorts prefer to spend the day out in the open, coming in at nightfall to feed in the shallows. As light is vitally necessary to see where to shoot, the wildfowler must follow them in the open, and this is where his skill receives its test. One of the objects of this chapter is to explain the art of the wildfowler, and I think that can best be accomplished by a description of an excursion in quest of wildfowl.

Heavy weather during the past few days has driven inland to the flooded Ings hundreds of fowl of many species. Morning dawns, calm, frosty and misty, and as the lightening grey dispels the dark shadows of the passing night, the low-lying, cigar-like punt, with its grim gun barrel pointing forwards, is propelled by even strokes of the "creeping sticks," skilfully operated by the recumbent fowler. Through the thin sheets of crisp, crackling ice, on goes the punt towards a distant and partly-submerged bank, from which arises the varied but not unmusical chatter of many wildfowl. Duck, widgeon, golden and green plover, and other wading birds are all here—while overhead some geese "honk" to one another, as they wing their way towards the distant Humber with measured beats of their powerful wings. So still is the morning that the air-rush at each downstroke of their mighty pinions is plainly heard, although the great birds are high out of gunshot, and as yet quite indistinguishable. The water laps gently against the bows of the punt, and the "crishing" ice sounds to the strained ears of the fowler loud enough to awaken the dead, much more the wary and not far-distant fowl. A redshank, disturbed at the bank behind the fowler, flies screeching past, and misses by a hair's breadth detecting the leaden grey punt. The cripple stopper is released from the fingers which grasp it, which have waited for the redshank's alarm note to take dire vengeance on this would-be spoiler of a shot amongst the bankful of fowl. Away in the distance, the dull report of a gun breaks through the mist, and presently the whirling wings and "wheohs" of widgeon betoken the approach of a "paddling" of these birds, at which the gun has probably been discharged, and which soon proceed to join their comrades on the bank. Closer and closer creeps the shadowy punt, until barely forty yards separate fowler from fowl ; each moment the light grows stronger and the mist begins to lift. Presently round lumps loom up ahead, and, straining his eyes, the fowler can detect one, two, three duck—then more and more—until the gun is trained upon the thickest portion of the clustering flock, now busily engaged spattering about in the half-frozen mud. The suspense grows greater every instant. "Don't shoot yet," is the prompting of experience ; while excitement cries, "Let 'em have it." Cool judgment conquers ; the itching trigger-finger holds the lives of many fowl in the balance, and as the last clinging mist wraith lifts, and discloses to the frightened eyes of the "squattering" birds the grim outline of the deadly gun punt, a shrill alarm note rings out, as, with one accord, duck and dunlin, pochard and plover, spring into the air with a mighty clatter of wings and splashing of water. Crash goes the big gun amid a huge cloud of grey smoke, and the charge of heavy shot tears a ragged hole through the centre of the rising fowl. Plip, plop, splash, go dunlin, plover and duck. Fowl rain down in response to the deadly call, and the punt shoots forward among the dead and dying birds, clear of the cloud of smoke, where the increasing light enables the cool-nerved fowler to wield his hand-gun with precision among the cripples that, winged or pricked, scuttle off in every direction. Gradually the echoes die away, the water laps slower as it smooths out after the momentary disturbance, the faint acrid smell of gunpowder grows fainter, and except for the slight rustle made by the old man collecting his spoil, quiet reigns once more.

When all is gathered in he picks up the paddle (there is no need to lie flat in the punt for a time, as the shot has effectually scared all the wildfowl in the vicinity), and propels his punt across the wide expanse of water towards a clump of willows, a likely place for a "spring" of teal to be floating at ease after their heavy night-feeding, the first food they have taken since the storm of the day before. In such case they are likely to be tired and easily approached, and, sure enough, in the lee of the osier patch float half a dozen feathery balls, victims of Morpheus ; heads tucked under blue-barred wings, all unconscious of approaching danger. Thus they offer an easy chance to the fowler, whose living depends on his success in destroying these sleepy birds, and he does not scruple to avail himself of it. Probably they never wake up at all, for in response to the crash of the big gun, the whole half-dozen are lifted into the air by the impact of the heavy shot, and, falling back again, quite dead, are soon picked up and added to the result of the previous fusillade. The winter sun glints upon a million hoar crystals, and lights up the water so that every little chip of flotsam and jetsam stands out sharp and clear.

Here and there huge patches of open water gleam conspicuously, and smaller open rings within the ice show where companies of fowl have swum round the night long, to keep an open space beneath the Ice King's solidifying breath. A slight blue haze curls upwards from the red roof-pots of yonder cottage, and at the sight the pole is wielded with longer strokes, the little craft shoots forward with its dead and living burden, towards the home comforts heralded by the filmy smoke-wreaths, and across the silent expanse of flood and pasture, the silvery chime of a distant church clock proclaims the flight of time. And now he ceases his venery until the falling of the shades of even call him once more to embark in his frail craft to pit his skill against the wild nature of the wariest of God's creatures.

Such is a description of an actual wildfowling excursion with punt and big gun. I could give hundreds of details as to the result of such expeditions, but I am afraid such facts and figures would become too wearisome to my readers, no matter how keen they might be on wildfowling. It may not be out of place to state that even a case-hardened fowler like Snowden Slights feels his pulses quicken on certain red-letter days in the calendar of sport. Who amongst us who have tried our 'prentice hands but would like to experience the thrills which doubtless passed through the old man's heart during the two best consecutive days' shooting he ever had in all his successful career, for on this memorable occasion he was successful in gathering ninety-nine ducks between Monday morning and Tuesday night. At another time, with the twenty-third shot of the season,

E

made with the punt-gun in 1895, he secured twenty-nine ducks and three pochard. Also during the year, the thirty-second shot resulted in killing the second largest number of duck ever secured by Slights. With a single shot he accounted for twenty-four ducks and sixteen widgeon, a total of forty. Truly a magnificent shot !

Indeed, the old wildfowler made a series of fine shots during that year, and amongst a long list of good ones, there is another which stands out prominently. It was the fifty-seventh shot of the season, made in Wheldrake Ings, his favourite punting-ground, and resulted in thirty-six ducks being brought to bag. I have remarked upon the large numbers of green plover which frequent the Ings, and have also commented upon the big shot once made at them. There are many others which are worthy of notice, but I will conclude this chapter by mentioning two only, the fifty-sixth and fifty-seventh punt-gun shots of the year 1900, which resulted in a score of thirty-three and thirty-two green plover respectively.

CHAPTER VIII.

REMINISCENCES.

E ARLY winter floods had attracted large numbers of
fowl from the sea-coast. They love to frequent such
spots, in order to cleanse themselves thoroughly
from the sea lice that swarm upon their bodies and
which the fresh water readily helps to get rid of.
A big mass of birds were congregated out in the open,
practically secure from harm, thanks to the natural advantages of the place and their own cunning. Day after day
the old fowler looked at them through his field-glass, and
as often turned regretfully away, well knowing that as long
as such open weather continued, he would have no chance to
get near them ; but one morning, how different was the
scene ! A night's hard frost had gripped the top of the
water, the smooth surface being broken here and there into
open pools, showing where the fowl had ceaselessly swum
in circles in order to keep some open spaces, the centres of
which they occupied in disconsolate groups.

Several days passed ; the ice ever thickening, and the
wildfowl having hard work to keep their pools from closing
over, and still the old fowler awaited his opportunity. With

characteristic suddenness, a thaw set in, and presented Slights with his chance. Long before the dawn, he pushed off in his punt, guiding it skilfully along the lanes between the floating ice. Paddling and poling, he proceeded boldly amongst the grinding masses of ice that momentarily threatened to overwhelm his eggshell-like craft and precipitate the grim gun and human freight into the freezing water splashing so crisply under the bows. I may here state that floating ice is a source of considerable danger to the wildfowler, and on one occasion Snowden Slights was in the punt when a strong wind swept down upon him just at the moment the punt was in a tight place in the ice. The gust caused the ice-floes to close in and incidentally stave several strakes off the punt, causing it to instantly fill with water and sink beneath him. Luckily, he was fairly near the shore at the time of the accident, and also in a shallow place, otherwise he might not have been able to scramble out little the worse except for a ducking, the broken punt being recovered next day and the gun fished up from the bottom of the flood. Continuing steadily through the ice straight out into the midst of the frozen desolation, the grey dawn breaking slowly opposite the nose of the punt gradually shed sufficient light to silhouette the forms of some fowl a hundred yards ahead. So far they were all asleep, their heads cosily tucked under their wings. Probably it was only an after-dinner nap, for one wary old mallard stretched its neck and looked toward the punt—the crackling ice betrayed the approach of danger, but the puntsman, being in the shadow, stretched flat in his craft, could not be easily distinguished. Carefully he pushed forward with gentle strokes of his "creeping-sticks." Reassured, the mallard slept again ; the punt approached another ten yards. Then several duck "sensed"

A GOOD SHOT AT
GREEN PLOVER.

POACHER AND
LURCHER.

danger, and gazed anxiously around. The old man waited ; they settled again to their snooze, and he gained another ten yards. The big gun slewed across their centre—at fifty yards the alignment was perfect—a shrill whistle broke from the fowler's lips—the startled fowl spread wings, and sprang frantically into the air, the hammer dropped simultaneously, and the tremendous boom of the punt-gun rent the silence as its deadly charge sped in a desolating hail through the rising birds. A few whip-like cracks followed, as the cripple-stopper, guided by the steady hand and eye of the old wild-fowler, persuaded the winged duck to stay behind. The spoil was picked up and stowed beneath the punt-gun, and, as he counted them in, he realised that the biggest shot of his life-time was there represented, twenty-four heavy duck (mallard) and twenty widgeon, a total of forty-four duck at one shot, and such an one as his father had talked of as possible in the palmy days of wildfowling.

Rather more than twenty years ago, a winter of the old-fashioned sort brought thousands of fowl out of their Northern fastnesses, and distributed them over the country. At night it was so cold that it was impossible to be out of doors more than an hour at a time, and a number of poor people were found frozen to death in various parts of York-shire and the North. One week in January, the old fowler commenced operations with his favourite sport. Pushing off in his punt, he traversed several ice channels, or had covered a distance of about a mile, when he made out a little bunch of pochard* under the lee of a bank. He saw there was only one way by which he could get near them, and that meant a long paddle right round to the back of the bank. This

---

(*) A species of small diving duck.

he essayed and eventually accomplished, and the pochard were found to be nicely within shot. But as the bank was very high, the big gun had to be lifted out of the punt and dragged to the top, and a risky shot taken over the edge of the bank. After a good deal of struggling with his heavy burden, and fearful the whole time lest the birds should hear the noise he was compelled to make and to take alarm, he got the barrel over and took sight at his quarry. Steadying himself a moment, and kicking his toes deeply into the bank, he pressed the trigger. The usual mighty report followed, and the recoiling gun moving quickly and relentlessly against Slights' shoulder, proved to be a great deal more powerful than he had bargained for. But as he discovered that fact, he was already tumbling backward, with the gun after him, into the icy waters of the Derwent, causing a huge splash as he disappeared into a depth of five or six feet. Hastily scrambling out, he got into the punt, and, wringing wet, went to retrieve his birds, securing four, three winged ones escaping, owing to the impossible task of giving chase when clad in rapidly-freezing garments.

At once he made for home (two miles away). How he arrived, he does not remember. He certainly had one of the "closest calls" of his life ; he could not speak, and his hard-frozen clothes had to be cut off by his friends. To this day he clearly recalls the agony of returning life to his frozen limbs, but, thanks to an iron constitution, he was next day again able to follow his calling. For a week succeeding this adventure, he never had time to change his clothes. Night and day he was out in pursuit of fowl ; the tremendously keen weather being exceptionally favourable for the successful following of his calling. So near home were the fowl that he could nearly shoot them from his doorstep, and could thus alternate between fowling and brief intervals for refreshment, only sparing himself from his arduous toil to snatch three hours' sleep each evening. This incident occurred years before he thought of keeping a record of his bags, and the whole red-letter time is therefore nothing but a memory. I was never able to glean anything like an exact total result of this great event, the old fowler's memory not being equal to the task, but he estimates he secured several hundreds of fowl, and has never shot so many before or since.

It is only natural that a fine shot like Snowden Slights should on occasion be called upon to tests of skill among his friends; and at local pigeon-shooting matches he has disposed of twenty or more birds without a miss.

Some years ago he formed one of a rabbiting party at Thicket Priory, but not wishing to monopolise the sport, intended principally for the other guns, he stood in the line with his old muzzle-loader, and watched the shooting. There were four guns besides his own, and directly the rabbits were on the move, the old wildfowler (when all four had unsuccessfully finished firing at them) was given the task of stopping the quarry. Almost without exception the party missed the scurrying bunnies, and not until they were at least seventy yards away did the old man get his chance. Yet, I have it on undoubted authority, that not a rabbit escaped that he fired at, and thus did yeoman service in compiling a good bag.

Slights does not approve of shooting for wagers, and it was with great reluctance that he was once drawn into contesting a match against another gunner, noted more for his ability as a braggart than as a good shot. The test was to be the shooting of five pigeons and five sparrows, both at twenty-five yards rise. The challenger shot first, his score being one pigeon out of five. Slights then grassed four birds inside the boundary, and one bird fell just outside ; the sparrows were not fired at, as the discomfited sportsman paid up, and left the ground without further remark.

Chatting one day to the old fowler on various topics, the talk veered round to the subject of dreams, and he related several of his experiences on this head, two of which may be of interest. In fancy he was occupied cutting a patch of three-year-old osiers at Sutton, using the peculiar sickle-bladed knife generally adopted for that purpose. Presently he heard the soughing and rush that could only be caused by passing geese, and, looking upwards, he saw a party of these great birds flying straight towards him. In a few moments they passed over his head, so low that they barely cleared the tops of the willows. The opportunity was irresistible, and with a quick flirt of his hand, he flung the willow-knife at the leading goose, and to his unbounded surprise cut its head clean off. With a crash it fell down upon him—and he woke to find his grandson standing over him, asking, "What are you malling out for, grandad? Did you tummle out er bed?" "He would have malled out, too, if he could have had the same feeling in his ribs as I had," drily remarked the old fowler. On another occasion Slights dreamed he was wending his way along the river-bank near Ellaughton, with his gun under his arm, when he espied five ducks flying straight over his head. Drawing a bead upon the leader, he pulled the trigger, and knocked four of the flock down, and it was only when he had got across the bedroom floor and bumped his head against the opposite wall that he realised that his quarry only existed in his very lively imagination.

The old fowler is wonderfully optimistic, and possesses a very keen sense of humour. Some of my readers will remember that in his old age Slights was prostrated for almost a year with the only serious illness of his life, and, in common with his medical man, we had all given up hope of seeing him about again. In company with a friend, I was sitting by his bedside, and we were both trying to cheer the patient up a little. In this laudable endeavour my friend related to him a piece of news concerning a lock-keeper over whose head eighty-two summers had passed, but who the previous week had taken to wife a blushing bride of twenty-five. My friend jokingly suggested to the wildfowler that he would be soon doing likewise, and was somewhat surprised by the reply, "I don't know for certain, gentlemen, I'll see how I feel next week!"

Occasionally he launches out as a story-teller, and here is a sample of his anecdote. A waggoner returning from Selby, finding the day warm and his throat dry, called at so many wayside hostels that night overtook him in the neighbour-hood of Ellerton, and having imbibed not wisely but too well, he became so helpless as to roll from his waggon into the grass by the roadside, and was discovered fast asleep by a number of young farm hands who recognised him. The horses had stood patiently awaiting the will of their driver, and the young fellows, seeking to take a rise out of the waggoner, released the traces, and turned them into an adjacent field, leaving the man to sleep peacefully on. The village policeman going his rounds next found the slumberer, and, shaking him roughly, obliged him to give an account of himself. Rubbing his eyes and gazing about him stolidly, the waggoner said: "If my name is Bill Johnson, I have lost two horses. If it is not—well, then, I have found a waggon!''

Not the least of the dangers to which the wildfowler is exposed is the risk of being shot by another puntsman, and in this connection Snowden Slights relates an instance of a narrow shave he once had of losing his life. It occurred in this wise. He had approached very close to a paddling of widgeon, and was lying in the lee of a low bank, which was awash with the water, when he descried the punt of another fowler approaching the quarry from a direction on a diagonal with his own, and who was awaiting an opportunity to place a deadly and exterminating charge. At this juncture the widgeon rose, and again alighted, but midway between the approaching punt and himself, thus offering the other fowler a splendid chance to pull off a good shot. Luckily, the full distance between the punts was fairly long (about 100 yards), otherwise our friend would never have lived to relate the adventure. He had just time to see the inevitable, and to stretch himself flatter still along his punt-bottom, and the next instant a liberal quantity of B.B. shot crashed into the planking, some passing through the light gunwale and stinging the old man's body pretty sharply before they dropped, spent, on the bottom boards. Both puntsmen were, perhaps, too frightened to indulge in much recrimination, and each congratulated himself that matters were no worse. One of them, I know, profited by the narrow escape, as he is constantly advising my shooting friends "always to look where the shot is likely to reach before pulling trigger."

By bearing this advice in mind and acting upon it, one recognises a possible danger almost instinctively, and, if wise, refrains from loosing off, whether it be a heavy punt-gun or more insignificant, but none the less deadly, "hand" gun.

I will conclude this chapter by a reference to Snowden Slights' grandfather, a rugged character who died the same week that Snowden was born. There is an old eight-bore single-barrelled muzzle-loader in the armoury that was his property at the time he resided on the Yorkshire Wolds, near Pocklington, and which was paid for as the result of one shot at a "stand" of dotterill. A naturalist would envy the old veteran the sight of such a flock as large as that which he must have secured. What sacrilege it was to shoot them, none but a bird-lover can realise! To get sight of half a dozen nowadays is luck indeed, but at that time, namely, the early part of the nineteenth century, dotterill were both plentiful and cheap, and guns very expensive. To put the value of the gun as low as five pounds, and dotterill at a wholesale price of two shillings each (this latter a figure probably far more than they would actually realise), it means that that single shot knocked out fifty specimens of a bird now valued so highly that one only constitutes a prize to the present-day naturalist sportsman.

CHAPTER IX.

PUNT-GUN SHOTS AND AVERAGES.

IN a previous chapter I have already remarked how unfortunate it is that the old wildfowler has not kept a complete record of his shots. Such lists would probably be dry reading enough for the general reader but vastly interesting to the modern wildfowler and naturalist. There is, however, some reason for congratulation that figures are obtainable which cover a period of seventeen consecutive years, but lack of space prevents my publishing full details of punt-gun shots, even were they necessary, so I will confine my attention to the best, and the worst seasons only of the period alluded to. This will suffice for all purposes of comparison, as the totals given in the table of averages will supply the figures for the remaining seasons.

The first column of the table denotes the respective shots of the season in progressive order ; the second describes the quantity and species of the wildfowl obtained as the result of the shot ; and the third column gives the locality where the shot was fired. The lists, both of details and analysis, refer only to punt-gun shots, no record whatever having been kept of shooting done with the "hand-gun." Where

CREEPING
QUIETLY ALONG
A DYKE

FRONT VIEW OF
FLIGHT SHOOTING
SCREEN.

species like snipe, curlew, dunlin, shoveller, starlings, gulls, pigeons, etc., figure, it does not imply that such species are rare, neither does it imply they have been singled out as a mark for the big gun.

In a bad light gulls have generally been mistaken for duck, and other birds have fallen victims along with nobler quarry just because they happened to be in the way of the shot. Birds like shovellers and goosanders would be shot with the punt-gun, if it was impossible to get near enough to slay them by other means, but, as a general rule, the old fowler got as many fowl grouped for a shot as it was practicable to cover with his ponderous weapon. The following is a detailed account of the best season of which there is any record, that of 1892, and is followed by one of the worst, the latter, of course, being selected from a series, where the fowler was not prevented from following his occupation by ill-health, but by an unsuitable season and scarcity of wildfowl.

Shot.		Number and Description of Fowl.	Locality.
No.	1.	8 Green Plover.	Sutton.
,,	2.	20 ,,	Wheldrake.
,,	3.	3 Pochard.	Aughton.
,,	4.	11 Green Plover.	Ellerton.
,,	5.	4 Ducks and 1 Pochard.	Wheldrake.
,,	6.	13 Green Plover.	Wheldrake.
,,	7.	28 ,,	,,
,,	8.	29 ,,	,,
,,	9.	6 Gulls.	,,
,,	10.	1 Duck, 1 Widgeon, 9 Teal.	Bubwith.
,,	11.	6 Widgeon.	,,
,,	12.	21 Green Plover.	Wheldrake.
,,	13.	2 Pochard.	Bubwith.

Shot. No.		Number and Description of Fowl.	Locality.
No.	14.	28 Green Plover.	North Hills.
,,	15.	21 ,,	Wheldrake.
,,	16.	16 ,,	Bubwith.
,,	17.	14 ,,	North Hills.
,,	18.	39 ,,	Bubwith.
,,	19.	38 ,,	Ellerton.
,,	20.	9 Pochard.	E. Cottingwith.
,,	21.	5 Widgeon.	North Hills.
,,	22.	16 Green Plover.	Aughton.
,,	23.	15 ,,	,,
,,	24.	9 Teal, 5 Widgeon.	Wheldrake.
,,	25.	28 Green Plover.	Wheldrake Carrs.
,,	26.	3 Ducks.	Wheldrake.
,,	27.	1 Duck, 1, Teal, 6 Widgeon.	,,
,,	28.	24 Green Plover.	Aughton.
,,	29.	6 Ducks.	Duffield Carrs.
,,	30.	11 Widgeon, 1 Teal, 1 G. Plover.	Wheldrake.
,,	31.	1 Pochard.	Aughton.
,,	32.	21 Green Plover.	,,
,,	33.	16 Green Plover.	Bubwith.
,,	34.	19 ,,	Wheldrake.
,,	35.	15 ,, 1 Widgeon.	,,
,,	36.	8 ,,	Aughton.
,,	37.	4 Teal.	Ellerton.
,,	38.	25 Green Plover.	,,
,,	39.	4 Ducks.	Aughton.
,,	40.	2 ,,	Bubwith.
,,	41.	5 ,,	E. Cottingwith.
,,	42.	23 Green Plover.	Wheldrake.
,,	43.	2 Ducks.	E. Cottingwith.
,,	44.	5 ,,	Ellerton.

Shot.		Number and Description of Fowl.	Locality.
,,	45.	6 Pochard.	Wheldrake.
,,	46.	16 Ducks.	E. Cottingwith.
,,	47.	16 Teal.	Ellerton.
,,	48.	8 Ducks.	,,
,,	49.	1 Snipe.	E. Cottingwith.
,,	50.	19 Ducks, 1 Widgeon.	,,
,,	51.	8 Ducks.	River Derwent.
,,	52.	2 ,,	Aughton.
,,	53.	0 (Miss).	Wheldrake.
,,	54.	4 Ducks.	Aughton.
,,	55.	2 ,,	Lutton Carrs.
,,	56.	1 ,,	Wheldrake.
,,	57.	3 ,,	Lutton Carrs.
,,	58.	9 ,,	,,
,,	59.	2 ,,	North Hills.
,,	60.	6 ,,	Aughton.
,,	61.	1 ,,	,,
.,	62.	3 ,,	,,
,,	63.	25 ,,	Wheldrake.
,,	64.	4 ,, 1 Pochard.	North Hills.
,,	65.	4 ,,	North Hills.
,,	66.	10 ,,	Ellerton.
,,	67.	3 Widgeon.	North Hills.
,,	68.	2 Teal.	Aughton.
,,	69.	2 Pochard.	Ellerton.
,,	70.	6 Ducks.	Wheldrake.
,,	71.	1 Swan.	,,
,,	72.	6 Pochard.	Ellerton.
,,	73.	2 Ducks.	E. Cottingwith.
,,	74.	1 ,,	Ellerton.
,,	75.	2 ,,	,,

SHOT.		NUMBER AND DESCRIPTION OF FOWL.	LOCALITY.
No.	76.	1 Duck.	Wheldrake.
,,	77.	4 Ducks.	,,
,,	78.	5 ,,	Aughton.
,,	79.	2 ,,　3 Teal.	,,
,,	80.	2 ,,	,,
,,	81.	0 (Miss).	Wheldrake.
,,	82.	5 Ducks.	Thorganby.
,,	83.	1 ,,	Aughton.
,,	84.	13 Widgeon.	Ellerton.
,,	85.	0 (Miss).	Wheldrake.
,,	86.	12 Ducks.	,,
,,	87.	2 ,,	Ellerton.
,,	88.	2 Pochard.	Aughton.
,,	89.	9 Ducks.	————
,,	90.	2 Swans.	Aughton.
,,	91.	3 Ducks.	E. Cottingwith.
,,	92.	2 ,,	,,
,,	93.	5 Pochard.	Ellerton.
,,	94.	8 Ducks.	Wheldrake.
,,	95.	1 ,,	Thorganby.
,,	96.	5 ,,	Ellerton.
,,	97.	2 Widgeon.	E. Cottingwith.
,,	98.	6 Ducks.	Wheldrake.
,,	99.	6 ,,	E. Cottingwith.
,,	100.	5 Pochard.	Wheldrake.
,,	101.	4 Ducks.	,,
,,	102.	1 ,,	,,
,,	103.	0 (Miss).	Ellerton.
,,	104.	0 (Miss).	,,
,,	105.	2 Ducks.	,,
,,	106.	2 ,,	Wheldrake.

SEASON 1902.

SHOT.		NUMBER AND DESCRIPTION OF FOWL.		LOCALITY.
No.	1.	7 Ducks.		Wheldrake.
,,	2.	5 ,,		,,
,,	3.	2 ,,		,,
,,	4.	2 ,,		,,
,,	5.	10 ,,		,,
,,	6.	15 Green Plover.		,,
,,	7.	2 Ducks.		North Hills.
,,	8.	15 Ducks.		Wheldrake.
,,	9.	2 ,,	4 Widgeon.	North Hills.
,,	10.	5 ,,	1 Widgeon.	,,
,,	11.	5 ,,	5 Goosanders.	Wheldrake.
,,	12.	2 ,,		,,

Appended is the analysis of the total figures from 1890 to
1907, a period of eighteen years in all, but as the account
for 1904 cannot be traced it is of necessity omitted.

MALLARD, CALL DUCK, AND WILD DUCK.

F

ANALYSIS OF PUNT-GUN SHOTS FROM 1890 TO 1907.

Year	Ducks	Green Plover	Widgeon	Teal	Pochard	Pintail	Swans	Geese	Golden Plover	Snipe	Dunlin	Curlew	Shovellers	Starlings	Gulls	Goosanders	Pigeons	Coots	Total	Shots	Average
1890	398	78	54	24	24	1	11	5		1	17			67					680	71	9·7
1891	244	102	32	24	13			2				2			6				419	95	4·4
1892	257	517	54	45	43		3		12	1									926	106	8·7
1893	183	78	22	35	37	1		8	10				2						375	80	4·6
1894	166	224	63	10	25	1	2						2						501	93	5·3
1895	312	151	49	13	18				12		2								546	61	8·9
1896	96	29	14																79	13	6·07
1897	76	48	1	39	3					1					13				188	34	5·5
1898	87	18	40	3	8														145	36	4·0
1899	193		11		4	1	2	2							8		4		102	26	3·9
1900	105	121	59	18	20					1			2			3			429	59	7·2
1901	55	16	1	2															129	29	4·4
1902	83	15	5	29	4	1		6											78	12	6·5
1903		236	34																403	48	8·4
1904	81							1		4											
1905	68	10	0	3	7			1		4									99	19	5·2
1906	10	29	6	13	18								2						121	27	4·5
1907		83	9									1						2	135	21	6·4
Total	2434	1755	454	261	224	5	18	25	34	12	19	3	8	67	27	3	4	2	5355	830	6·4

Number of misses 19.

Average of effective shots 811 = 6·6.

PRICES OF WILDFOWL.

The quality of the wildfowl shot by Snowden Slights has been, and is, very good. Ducks are, of course, the principal item, and as they are considerably improved in value for the table by sojourning on fresh water, the old wild-fowler has always been successful in obtaining the best prices for them (as well as for other species of wildfowl) which he has sent to the York and Leeds markets. A perusal of the following paragraph will astonish some of our sea-going friends of the wildfowling fraternity.

Brent Geese, 2/6 each ; Bitterns, 2/- each ; Curlews, 1/3 each ; Coots, 6d. to 9d. each ; Cormorants, nil ; Crake (Spotted), 6d. ; Ducks (Mallard), 2/-, 2/3, and 2/6 each ; Divers (Red-throated), 2/6 each ; Dotterill, 6d. each ; Field-fares, 2d. to 3d. each ; Geese (White-fronted, Pink-footed, etc.), 2/- and 3/6 each ; Goosanders, 1/- to 2/- each ; Grebe (Little), 6d. each ; Grebe (Great Crested), 3/6 each ; Gulls, 4d. and 6d. each ; Golden-eye Duck, 2/- to 2/6 each ; Gadwall Duck, 1/6 each ; Godwits, 1/- each ; Green-shanks, 8d. each ; Herons, 1/- each ; Hawks, 6d. each ; Knots, 6d. each ; Kingfishers, 1/- each ; Larks, 1d. and 1½d. each ; Moorhens, 6d. each ; Ouzel (Water), 3d. each ; Pochard, 1/- each ; Pintail Duck, 1/9 to 2/6 each ; Plover (Grey), 6d. to 1/6 each ; Plover (Golden), 9d. to 1/- each ; Plover (Ringed), 6d. each ; Redshanks, 6d. to 9d. each ; Redwings, 2d. each ; Ruffs and Reeves, 6d. each ; Stilt, nil ; Scoters, 2/3 each ; Snipe (Jack), 4d. to 6d. each ; Snipe (Common), 6d. each ; Starlings, 1½d. to 2d. each ; Smew, 2/- each ; Stints (?) (Dunlin), 1½d. to 2d. each ; Shellducks, 2/6 to 5/- each ; Shovellers, 1/9 to 2/6 each ; Stockdoves (?) (Ringdoves), 5d. each ; Sandpipers, 6d. to 9d. each ; Swans (Bewick's), 5/- each ; Swans (Whooper),

6/6 and 7/- each ; Teal, 1/- each ; Tufted Ducks, 1/- each ; Widgeon, 1/- each ; Water-rail, 6d. each.

Many of these prices are of considerable interest ;   I wonder what some of our bird-collectors nowadays would give for a black-winged stilt obtained in Britain, an item for which Snowden Slights could not obtain a price? Ruffs and reeves at sixpence each are remarkably cheap, as also are bitterns at two shillings. Such figures form striking contrasts to the good prices he had for the various species of ducks.

Before the passing of the Wild Birds Protection Act, it was possible to shoot wildfowl for about six months of the year, and it was only at this time that the pursuit of wild-fowling as a commercial proposition in the Derwent Valley was really worth following. At this time the nett result of the six months' work generally averaged about £40, and the best season our old friend can recollect left a balance of £90 after all costs of licences, powder and shot, and incidentals had been paid. The shooting season to-day is of four months' duration, but even with a less number of days to average, the totals are nothing like what they used to be in past days when wildfowl were more amenable to being approached and shot. Of course, the flight of time has left its mark upon Snowden Slights, and one cannot now give figures that would offer fair comparison. The season just closed has been fairly favourable, and no doubt, if he had been a younger man, he would have secured a good number of ducks. As it is, however, he has fired the big gun eleven times, two shots missed the quarry, and nine were effective, and after deducting expenses of the shooting only, the result is a balance of one penny per diem.

BACK VIEW OF FLIGHT SHOOTING SCREEN.

DECOYS FOR
GREEN PLOVER

CHAPTER X.

FLIGHT-SHOOTING, FLIGHT-NETTING, AND SHOOTING OVER DECOYS.

THERE are one or two natural conditions upon which successful flight-shooting is absolutely dependent ; that is to say, the wildfowl must arrive in goodly numbers, and when appearing inland, the locality must be one that compels the flocks of birds to adopt certain lines of flight.

On the coast, the action of the tides in automatically flooding and receding from the haunts of wildfowl necessitates their being constantly to and fro on the wing. On the seaboard, the various species of ducks and geese spend the daylight hours sleeping, or, at any rate, quietly amusing themselves out on the open sea, and such is their wariness that they usually manage to keep all possible sources of danger at such a distance as to ensure their own safety. As night falls, the fowl assemble in flocks, and, rising off the water, come inland with marvellous speed, oft-times travelling many miles to feed upon the upland pastures and stubbles. This they do all night long, and they fly back again to the sea in the early morning, just before and at daybreak. In those haunts of wildfowl lying inland, the flight is governed by the suitability of the locality, the absence of molestation, and the food supply. On the wide expanses of flooded Ings at East Cottingwith, the ducks are able to spend the day in comparative peace out on the open water, and it is practically impossible to get at them except by the aid of the gun-punt.

When they desire to feed, they must either approach the edges where the water is but a few inches deep, or leave the ings altogether, and fly either to Skipwith Common or to the stubbles and pastures of the surrounding country. As it would naturally be very unsafe to do this during the day-time, they are perforce obliged to fly off at night-fall, and spend the hours of darkness in satisfying the cravings of their stomachs ; and as it is quite the natural habit of ducks to feed at night, they do not experience any hardship. Unless the district is covered with ice and snow, they will "flight" every evening away from the open water, and return again just before the dawn to spend the day. When their feeding grounds are frozen up, the ducks have to keep an open space in the ice by constantly swimming round, and they will often go without food for several days under such circumstances. It is at the break-up of the ice after such a period, that wild-fowl fall the easiest prey, but if the frost has been very prolonged, the birds have become so thin that they are hardly worth shooting, or perchance they have left the dis-trict to go to the sea, until such times as their usual haunt is habitable once more.

A good deal of flight-shooting is done in the Derwent Valley by farmers and their men, but, as a rule, to little purpose. Snowden Slights himself detests flight-shooting, which feeling is very natural when one takes into consider-ation that it makes the ducks as wild as hawks, being so constantly harassed. The result is, the flocks are most difficult to approach in the punt after they have undergone a few experiences of being "blazed" at from every bit of cover over which they have had to pass.

They come over very high, more often fifty yards out of range of the concealed gunner than five yards within shot, and it is a moot point in the district whether more than one shot out of fifty is successful in bringing down a bird. The old wildfowler, in decrying flight-shooting, invariably requests his hearer to liken himself to a duck, but in this wise. "Suppose," he says, "you were going home to-night, and when you opened the front-door there was somebody standing behind it armed with a big stick, with which they fetched you a big crack on the head? You would look out for trouble, wouldn't you, the next time you had to open the door ; and it's the same with the ducks. I just get them 'haunted' about, and then the flight-shooting practically ruins everything. I have seen times when I could have shot numbers at flight, but I have not done it. I knew quite well that it would completely spoil the punting for several weeks."

Punting does not seem to have the same demoralising effect upon the ducks as flight-shooting ; maybe the reason is that they had settled down before a punt-gun was fired at them, whereas at flight, they were but on their way to their destination, and with every sense strained to watchfulness, they are far more ready to take notice of disturbances and attacks than they would be if allowed to settle in repose for a time.

During fine open weather, the fowl flight to and from the feeding and resting haunts, often at a tremendous height, and I have seen them drop to the water from over the middle of the ings almost from the clouds ; practically at no part of their flight-line were they ever within shot. This was the result of being so often fired at, and also partly on account of their natural habits. Heavy gales and storms cause them to fly low and near the ground ; sometimes they come over barely missing the tops of the flight-screens that may have been erected to receive them. At such times a good shot can take a heavy toll from the passing flocks, but opportunities such as these are rare, and when one has had the luck to seize upon such a chance, it is a red-letter entry for the diary. To be a good flight-shooter, one requires the possession of quick ears and eyes, steady nerves, and the ability to take shots at any angle at birds that pass at express speed. Successful flight-shooters are born, not made. I know no more hopeless task for the amateur wildfowler than the knocking over of birds which go over lightly as butterflies, but almost with the speed of light.

Snowden Slights used to be an excellent flight-shot and could knock over his quarry with consistent regularity, but it was only in exceptional circumstances that he was induced to pursue a sport for which he had so little sympathy. It is, of course, obvious that the flight-shooter should be well screened from the view of the approaching wildfowl, and flight-screens are constructed from all sorts of materials.

On the shore it is usual to sink a cask to its rim in the mud (midway under the line of flight), a portion of the knocked-out head coming in useful to make a seat inside it, then with a half a loggin of straw to make it comfortable one can get inside, light a pipe, and await the passing of the fowl with a fair degree of comfort. The only drawback to such shelters is, they are apt to get filled with rain-water or by a high tide, and one does not enjoy stepping into a cask of icy-cold water in the grey of the morning, as the result of taking it for granted that the cask would be just as you had left it on the previous evening. It is well to have an old tin baler handy for use on such occasions.

In the Derwent Valley the flight-shooter is content to fix up a hurdle interlaced with furze-bush cuttings, to build a butt out of blocks of turf, such as the one forming the subject of our illustration, or even to ensconce himself in an angle of a hedgerow. Whatever screen is erected, it is of vital importance that it should not be conspicuous, and the fowl should be allowed to pass over it for some time before shooting is commenced. For it is surprising what little differences in the contour of the country over which the flight takes place will cause the birds to sheer off just out of range the moment before the waiting gunner was going to shoot.

The best flight-shooting in the district is at green plover. These birds generally come off the fallows at dusk, and appear to delight in skimming the surface of the water, or flying in huge circles at no great height above it. They travel at a great rate, much faster, in fact, than is apparent, and to shoot them it is necessary to give the gun plenty of lead—indeed, very often two or three yards is none too much. Green plover have the location of the almost submerged banks quite "pat," and they love to resort to them for the purpose of cleansing the clay of the fallows from their feet. I have often gone out in the punt to one of these banks, and between dusk and darkness succeeded in bagging from ten to twenty of these birds, every one offering the most sporting shot any lover of the gun could possibly desire.

FLIGHT-NETTING.

The Derwent Valley does not offer suitable advantages for the practice of flight-netting. It is more than thirty years ago since Snowden Slights bent his thoughts upon nets, as being likely to be useful to him in the pursuit of his calling, but as he was unable to gather any information in the district concerning their size, the methods of erection, and other necessary details, he was faced with the necessity of journeying to some distant place where he could see the nets in operation. Eventually he heard that flight-nets were used at a certain place in Lincolnshire, and thither he repaired, travelling a good part of the way on a keel, which plied up the Derwent from Hull, its skipper giving him a lift also on the return journey.

On arrival at the little village, the old wildfowler was disappointed to find that the men who owned the nets would only part with their information at a fee of five pounds, a sum of money far too much to ask, he considered for such a trivial matter.

After wasting several days, and being no nearer his goal, the netsmen not following their calling as long as he was in the vicinity, he decided to gain his end by strategy. Giving out that he was going home on the morrow, but first having discovered the place where the flight-nets were usually erected, he ostensibly went away, and then following a roundabout route made his way to the place where the nets ought to be. He spent the night and most of the next day in hiding, but was rewarded at last by observing the whole process of the erection of the nets.

Returning home, he set to work, and made a range of nets, which he ultimately set up in what he took to be a suitable locality, but was disappointed to find they did not catch wildfowl in anything like the number caught by the professional netsmen. The reasons for his failure are not far to seek. Where there are wide stretches of open saltings, like those fringing various sections of our coasts, such localities offer ideal facilities for the erection of flight-nets; the birds are in great numbers, and they follow certain well-defined routes, and these conditions render it possible to intercept them with a fair amount of certainty, as they invariably fly low, in fact, barely clear of the "slob" (mud) ; and if the nets are set by a skilled man, the hurtling flocks dash straight into the meshes.

In the Derwent Valley, the fowl usually fly low only under exceptional circumstances—for instance, during a gale of wind accompanied by sleet or snow. Probably nine nights out of ten, they go right up in the sky for all the world like large winged champagne bottles. This just describes the appearance of flighting duck. Arrived at that portion of the ings where they wish to alight, they drop from the clouds straight to the water, and where is the chance to catch them in a flight-net? A flight-net may be anything from sixty yards to a quarter of a mile in length, is generally meshed six inches, and extends a width of ten to twenty feet. The one made by Snowden Slights is about eighty yards long, is a six-inch mesh, and ten feet high. It is erected to hang loosely from poles placed in the ground, twelve to fifteen yards apart, the site chosen being a narrow strip of land running out into the flooded ings, or a bank over which the fowl have recently been in the habit of flighting.

If the net is stretched taut, any fowl that strike it are only hurled back or out of the net as though from a spring, but by allowing it to hang loosely, even such small creatures as dunlin and snipe become hopelessly enmeshed, although the meshes are wide enough to allow such small fry to pass through quite readily.

Dark nights are the most suitable for flight-netting, as

darkness causes the wildfowl to fly low, and also renders the net invisible. Green plover are the most frequent victims, while large numbers of gulls and small waders have also been ensnared, ducks proving far too wary to be caught by this artifice except in one or two instances. Widgeon are marvellously fast birds on the wing, and a flock of these handsome duck has on two occasions struck the net and passed clean through, leaving nothing but a huge rent to mark their progress. Eventually the old wildfowler arrived at the conclusion that flight-netting on paying lines was impracticable in his district, and the nets were relegated to a distant corner of his storeroom, whence I unearthed them recently for the purpose of taking a photograph. Maybe that was the last time they will ever appear in public.

DECOYS.

The use of decoys to assist the wildfowler in securing his quarry has not yet become general in this country, much less in that part of it known as the Derwent Valley. Yet good decoys, skilfully placed, are most helpful ; one has only to look at those used in the shooting of wood-pigeons to see a successful adaptation of this method. Usually, decoys take the form of an artificial representation of the bird whose species it is desirable to attract, and such imitations may be made from a variety of substances. Wood, hollowed sheet-metal, and inflated india-rubber, coloured to a semblance of the natural object, are only some of the materials used. Stuffed birds may be adopted as decoys on land, and these are by far the best, the only objection being that they require to be carefully handled. They are costly to procure, unless home-made ; and last but not least, they do not endure, exposure to wind and rain completely destroying them. The same arrangements are made as for flight-shooting, with the

ONE END OF A FLIGHT NET.

DRAWING A
SALMON NET ON
THE DERWENT.

addition of a few artificial birds placed naturally about on
the water, in front of the "hide." The appearance of these
decoys may be considerably improved and made to be more
natural by placing a piece of lead below the body of the
decoy for ballast, and by attaching a string to each in such
a manner that, on being pulled, the decoy dives its head
under water in a most lifelike manner. Then if one foot is
placed through a loop at the end of the string, the hands
are left at liberty to use the gun when the whirring of wings
and the calls of birds announce the approach of a flock.

Such a party attracted by the bobbing decoys will lower
their flight, and swing near or over them, and thus give
the fowler a chance to secure a shot ; whereas, if he had
no decoys out, the passing fowl would often have continued
their ordinary course, and probably kept far out of gunshot.
Snowden Slights did not regularly pin his faith to the use
of decoys. I have previously stated that he detested flight-
shooting, but he was always open to try any method which
might assist him in his calling, and that accounts for the
sundry wooden duck decoys among his possessions. He
admits their successful if somewhat uncertain use ; they
help materially in the securing of sporting shots at the fowl
attracted, but as he states, "I do not shoot for sport as
much as for a living. I like the sport, but it must always
give place to pot-shots, if by a pot-shot I can secure more
fowl."

The old fowler always had a small party of semi-wild duck
about his cottage, a white "call" specimen being among
them to enable him to pick out his tame birds when far out
on the waste of waters around his home. On many occasions
this flock of natural decoys has attracted their wilder
brethren almost to the cottage door, and for this service

they earned their keep. As a rule, they became so used to the flash and noise of the big gun, that they hardly took any notice when Snowden Slights caused its destructive charge to make deadly havoc among some party of confiding fowl which his live decoys had lured quite near his house. The old fowler's grandson, the late Mr. Snowden Plaxton, a fine sportsman, was very fond of shooting green plover over wooden decoys, painted to represent the real birds. Some of the illustrations depict him following this sport. September and October are the best months for its pursuit ; the green plover are then in large flocks, and not having been greatly disturbed are the more easily decoyed. The lapwing, terefit, or peewit, as it is variously called, is not at best by any means a confiding bird ; it has a marvellous aptitude for the discovery of the wildfowler's flight-screens, and very often, when quite at a long distance, will turn off at a tangent, and leave the would-be shooter disconsolate.

Decoys should always be placed head to the wind, as this is the most natural pose, and the more that can be posed, the better chance will there be of good sport. They should also be placed in close proximity to the screen, as it is most likely that approaching quarry will endeavour to alight on the extreme edge of the party, and furthest from the shooter. I have seen Mr. Snowden Plaxton gather up thirty or more plover, after an evening's flighting over decoys ; and shooting from the same screen, I have several times assisted in the compiling of good bags.

Green plover offer most sporting shots, and when the night is shutting down, and darkness blotting from view the surrounding objects so useful to the gunner in judging distance, the consistent shooting of these apparently (only apparently) slow-winged birds is one of the best tests of skill I can conceive.

Of great assistance to the flight-shooter is the ability to "call" the various species of wildfowl ; a good "caller" will bring birds over one's head like hovering butterflies. Snowden Slights himself did not practise "calling," but several of my friends who could whistle the notes of curlews, knots, green, golden, and grey plover, and many other species, have often enjoyed good sport as the result of their skill in this direction.

I have seen a curlew whistled up from the bank a mile away, only to thump the mud in response to the charge of No. 5, which met him as he shrieked the answering note less than thirty yards from the butt. Again, birds like redshanks and knots will come over in response to a good "caller" so close as almost to knock off one's cap. The art of "calling" can easily be classed under the heading of "decoys," and if my advice is worth anything, let me say to the would-be wildfowler—Practise the calls of your quarry with all your might ; it is the most useful accomplishment you can possess when you go down to the shore. Also do not forget that shore birds have alarm notes as well as feeding notes, and love notes also, and it is of little use holding your gun in readiness for yonder distant curlews, the while you are straining your lungs in whistling their alarm notes.

In concluding this chapter, I may say that the wildfowler should never forget that the place he decides to make his flighting stand is but a speck compared with the area which the fowl will frequent. Hence its location requires most careful selection, and it is only by particular observation of the flight-lines of the fowl that such a spot may be decided upon.

In considering the wonderful grasp of the details of his craft possessed by Snowden Slights, one thing stands out paramount, namely, his marvellous skill in foretelling to a nicety where the fowl were to be found, and where they would come at a particular time. It is to this unerring knowledge that he owes in a great measure his success as a wildfowler.

CHAPTER XI.

SALMON AND EEL NETTING.

OF late years the pollution of the lower reaches of the Ouse below the mouth of the Derwent has played havoc with the immigration of that king of fishes, the salmon. When Snowden Slights was a young man the spring run of salmon could be looked forward to with some certainty, and also with the expectation that there would be a good number of fish. The deadly gush from the filth-laden channels of the Aire and Calder changed all this ; year after year the salmon swimming up against the sickening flood were swept back into the Humber, but then wrong side uppermost, grim testimony to the deadly efficiency of the poisonous ebb.

Strong efforts have been made by the Fishery Board to remedy this unfortunate state of affairs, and with some success, as is evidenced by the now-increasing number of fish (salmon) observed leaping at the various weirs, and by the fair proportion that are obtained by the netsmen at Naburn. When salmon were "running," the usual procedure was to fasten one end of the net to the bank by means of a stake, and then, after neatly arranging it in a good roomy boat, to pay out the net over the side, as the boat was sculled across the river and back again to the same side in a wide circle. This would result in paying out about eighty to one hundred yards of net twelve feet deep, and weighted on the lower edge with burnt clay sinkers, the upper edge being buoyed with discs of cork ; then, when the two ends were brought together, a large piece of water was completely enclosed. The net was now "wheeled" (the term used for "drawn in"), and the individual members of the catch were examined for retention, or rejection, according to their value. Numbers of pike were caught, as also were vast quantities of chub, roach and perch, and such coarse fish found a ready sale among the Jewish population in Leeds.

The old fowler's brother, James Slights, paid the most attention to the netting of salmon, and for several years was very successful. Big fish were never plentiful, and the largest obtained only weighed twenty pounds, but, as on most occasions when out netting, the catch made up in numbers what individually it lacked in weight. The work proved fairly profitable, and was only discontinued when the scarcity of salmon, owing to the river pollution, made the step inevitable. Blank hauls of the net were unusual, probably because the local knowledge of the netsmen led them to work just in the right place, and the best "draws" resulted in from six to ten salmon being taken, the largest "draw" securing twelve of these beautiful fish. The salmon nets are still in Slights' store-room, and have been kept in good order, although it is many years since they last made an appearance on the river bank, and, as far as he is concerned, it is unlikely they will be used again.

A few salmon are still taken at Sutton, and it is probable the fishery may be worth working again in a few years' time, as of late the spring "runs" have been fairly good, and are most certainly improving.

To take fish by netting them is a method despised by the rodsman ; such wholesale systems of capturing fish or game seldom finds favour with sportsmen, and I do not pretend to uphold netting as a "sport." Where, however, it is carried on as a business, or for the purpose of taking fish for re-stocking, it is a fascinating process to watch, and I have always found it most absorbing to stand by as the net is gradually drawn in, to see the first slight movements of net and water that denote some fish are enclosed— to mark the increasing disturbance, the frantic turmoil of the silvery gleaming mass, and then to help to sort large from small, useful from useless, and to return the rejected into the water. It is, too, most interesting to be able to examine such numbers as may be taken in a successful draw, as almost every variety the water contains may be collected into the net.

EEL NETTING.

It is surprising how little we know of the natural history of the eel, despite the researches of such eminent men as Petersen, Grassi, and others. Strictly speaking, a minute description of the eel and its habits (as far as these can be ascertained) does not come within the scope of this book ; I will, however, endeavour briefly to recount some of the chief features in the life of this slimy wriggler.

The eel is a pelagic spawner—that is, it spawns in the deep sea. Obviously it is oviparous, and for the purpose of depositing its eggs proceeds into the Atlantic, to a place about 300 miles from the Irish coast, where at a depth of three miles it performs those functions necessary for the continuance of its species. Young eels emerge from the ova as minute flattish and transparent creatures, known to science as "leptocephali," which follow out an instinct that compels them to proceed towards the river mouths, and by the time they have arrived there, they have reached the proportions of the elvers we know so well. Most of my readers have heard of, or seen, the "eel fare," or ascent of the elvers, i.e., countless millions of young eels ascending the river courses in a continuous army.

Years ago, before pollution had in a measure destroyed the fish-life of the rivers, all along the East Coast and in the Severn the ascent of the elvers used to be eagerly looked forward to by the poorer classes, who captured immense quantities of the young eels, and pressed them into a kind of jelly much esteemed as an article of food. Large numbers of elvers were caught, too, only to be devoted to the ignominious purpose of manuring land. Once settled among the mud and water weeds of our rivers, the elvers soon assume the proportions of "grigs," and also become the bane of the patient coarse-fish angler, who has every reason to curse them for their persistency in so gorging the tempting worms that covers his hook, that they have to be slit from end to end before it can be extracted.

It is now known that the sharp-nosed silver eel is the male, and the broad-nosed yellow eel the female ; their age may be ascertained by counting the concentric rings upon one of their scales (under a microscope), each group of five rings representing one year's growth. The males reach maturity at the age of four and a half to five years, and females from seven to ten years, and they stay in fresh water until that time, when, becoming ripe, they proceed down the rivers to their distant spawning grounds, from which, their life-work accomplished, it is thought they never return.

"WHEELING" IN
THE NET.

AN EEL NET.

There is considerable mystery surrounding these creatures; their presence in ponds, high up on moors, miles from any possible water connection with a river, has never been satisfactorily accounted for, although it is a well-known fact that eels can travel short distances overland. If anyone is desirous of proving how readily an eel will travel towards the nearest water when taken from its native element, he has only to procure a good lively specimen, and drop it in the middle of a field, when it will at once commence moving towards the nearest pond or stream.

Before leaving the subject to tackle the description of eel-netting, I may say that during the time the eels stay in fresh water, it is impossible to distinguish the sexes by the usual means, and it is exceedingly rare to find a female with undeveloped roe or ova ; in fact, it is only within the last two or three years that this has been done. Snowden Slights has told me that several times he has found eels with young inside them. This, in the ordinary course of nature, was an impossibility, and could only be accounted for by assuming that, like some other varieties of fish, they had, cannibal-like, swallowed their offspring. But it may be that Snowden Slights mistook some of the peculiar parasitic worms that tenant the body of the eel, for young. I well remember once catching a large eel that in its struggles exuded a worm about three inches long, which for a moment I myself took to be a young eel, and which specimen I still keep in spirits.

My photographs portray, better than any pen-picture, the long, wide-mouthed net, quickly tapering into a cane-hooped narrow cylinder, with an outside diameter of some twelve inches, the whole composed of strong finely-meshed twine. At the end the net tapers into a "purse" or "trap," which is in turn fastened at the extreme end by tying it together with twine. An eel or other fish, on entering the tunnel, speedily finds its way through the narrowing passage, until it arrives at the "purse," when the guiding funnel of mesh drops down behind it, and it would be a clever eel indeed that could pick up the loosely-hanging entrance to its prison walls.

A narrow stream, dyke, or cutting is usually chosen wherein to set the net, preferably one which the six-foot-round entrance will just span. Two stakes are driven into the sides of the stream to accommodate loops at the side of the net, and so keep it distended across the entire width, and to allow the cork floats to keep the rim just below the surface of the water—corresponding lead weights keeping down the lower edge.

It will thus be seen that the whole volume of water necessarily filters its contents through the net, and leaves behind in the "trap" any luckless fish which happens to be travelling with it. If the dyke is filled by tides, it is usual to drive another stake through a loop at the net-tail into the bed of the tideway, in order to prevent the flow from tangling the net into a shapeless and useless bundle of hemp. Fish can then easily pass over the net, and upstream with the tide, but are caught securely once they enter its yawning mouth with the ebb.

The usual contents of the "purse" consist of a squirming mass of eels, varied by occasional small pike and a few lampreys. Queer beggars, these lampreys, their seven breathing holes on each side of the neck giving the non-naturalist the impression of their having been struck through with a pronged fork ; and his sympathy deepens when closer inspection reveals the fact that the lamprey possesses no jaws like that of the eel, and has consequently to live by suction.

The best months of the year for eel-catching are, according to Snowden Slights, August and September. A warm, muggy evening during these months will make the eels turn out in full force, and fill the nets to overflowing. When I first described the old wildfowler's eel-net in the "Illustrated Sporting and Dramatic News," I received numerous letters of inquiry as to where such nets could be procured. I recommended a well-known fishing tackle firm as a possible source of supply, and I believe they made them for my correspondents. I find that Snowden Slights made his own nets, and he recently came across some notes on this subject, written on the inside cover of an old diary, but they are not quite complete. They pertain to an eel-net made for the beck, and I give the details here, as some of my readers may be able to make use of it :—

Set on sixty meshes for the tail, let out the first hoop five meshes, and net forty-five rounds between the hoops ; the top or weed hoop is rather larger than the others, and the mesh is let out ten meshes ; then let out a quarter to sixty meshes ; the rest of the net to its mouth should be let out each half-dozen rounds, until wide enough to span the creek it is required for. The mesh of these nets does not vary in size, and is worked on a half-inch mesh board.

Some years ago, Slights made his record catch for one night's work by taking thirty stones of eels by the aid of one net. I have no figures as to the number of fresh-water snakes that go to make up a take of eels like that, but if the average weight was half a pound (and that is placing it rather high) the total is eight hundred and forty. As in the case of wildfowl, he obtained a capital price for fish, and he never received less than sixpence per pound for both eels and lampreys.

CHAPTER XII.

LAMPREY AND EEL TRAPPING.

THE river lamprey or lampern (Petromyzon fluviatilis) ascends both the Ouse and the Derwent early in the spring for the purpose of spawning, and often in large numbers. During January and February, lampreys will take advantage of the heavy freshes to make their way over the otherwise almost insurmountable obstacles that exist in the shape of the various lock weirs. Once these obstructions are overcome, they travel upwards against the stream in a continuous procession, until they reach suitable gravelly shallows, whereon to deposit their ova previous to returning seawards, and, their mission in life accomplished, dying. They are weird-looking creatures, slimy of skin and scaleless ; a sucker in place of the orthodox mouth, and with seven breathing holes in the sides of the neck instead of the usual form of gill apparatus, and even the two dorsal fins are not paired ; while their food consists of any members of the small animal and insect communities.

Lampreys may often be seen attached by their sucker mouths to the flat of a stone below the surface of the stream, and if the hold be transferred to one's hand, the sensation is decidedly queer, and the sucker leaves an oval red mark to remind one of the incident for some hours.

For a long time young lampreys were understood to be a distinct species, and were known as "Ammococetes," so different are they to the adult. They have a different breathing mechanism, and the eyes are unexposed, and it is not until the third or fourth winter of their existence that they assume a mature appearance and grow to a length of from twelve to eighteen inches. The flesh of the lamprey is pink in colour when cooked, and is of a very rich flavour. In olden days lamprey pie was considered a "bonne bouche," and worthy the epicurean palate of a king. In fact, there is a legend that places the death of an English king (Henry I.) to the account of a lamprey pie.

At any rate, lampreys are good to eat, if one can overcome that sense of repugnance which appears to assail the appetite of many people when confronted with a dish of fresh-water snakes. I am afraid those fishermen who devote their attention to the capture of these creatures would not make a good lving if they depended upon the sale of their quarry as an article of diet for the people. Most of the lampreys caught in our rivers are sold to the Dutch line fishermen, and also to our own fishermen, to be used as bait for nobler fish, and the usual price commanded is about five pounds per thousand.

Snowden Slights found that the making of the special wicker traps or "lamprey baskets" was more profitable than using them, as the best place to set such traps was in the neighbourhood of some fishing weir, and these fishing grounds are let by the owners of the manor, or those who have the fishery rights. At such places, notably that at Naburn, a cutting was made from the higher to the lower water level, and fitted with sluice-gates to regulate the flow of the water. Along the course of this cutting, the baskets—

bottle-shaped wickerwork objects six feet long, and with a twelve-inch square entrance that filled the bottom of the culvert—were set, taper-end up stream, the wide mouth ready to welcome the lampreys as they progressed against the current through the channel towards the next level of the river. Once inside the basket, they were prevented from escaping by the *"chevaux de frise" that formed the guiding taper of the ingress to the trap ; but coming to a common centre in the body of the trap, exactly the same as in the case of an eel basket, the imprisoned fish found it impossible to get out again, and they were ultimately taken out by the fishermen emptying the trap from the NARROW end, where a wooden plug was fitted for that purpose.

The old wildfowler did not reside close enough to a weir to make it worth his while to rent fishery rights, and he was content to set a few baskets only in the river when the lampreys were running, and by this means he was successful in catching fair numbers, but nothing like as many as he caught at a part of the river that compels them to follow a particular and narrow route. In company with a friend I discovered a stretch of low-lying grass-land near the Derwent, literally covered with lampreys. It was during the month of February, and there had been a biggish flood that had evidently tempted them to leave the course of the river, and try to proceed round the weir and so continue their way up stream. This would have been all right (and maybe was, for a great many) had not the water fallen quickly, and left hundreds of lampreys swimming about in a couple of inches of water on the land. Of course, we filled our creels, and then proceeded into the adjacent village to borrow some fish-basses wherein to place our captures.

---

* Row of sharp points.

After securing four hundred, we tired of the business, and informed some of the "locals" of what was to be had ; upon which they promptly went forth to gather up the balance of lampreys we had left. Eventually we arrived home with a diminished bag, having given away a large number en route.

Setting aside a certain portion of our spoil for culinary experiments, we inflicted the rest upon unoffending relatives and friends, many of whom "blessed" us heartily later for giving them the trouble of preparing various little greasy-looking dishes, only to discover too soon that their fickle "little Marys" refused to accommodate them.

EEL TRAPPING.

Where rivers are too wide to permit of nets being used, or on ponds or lakes where there is no current, in order to capture eels in any quantity wicker "leaps" or "traps"— as they are variously called—are employed. By these means Snowden Slights has caught immense quantities of eels, and being a basket-maker, it naturally followed that he made all his "traps" himself. The interior economy of an eel-basket is simply formed by making a tapered tunnel-entrance to the trap itself, the sharp points of the end of the taper portion offering an invincible front to the luckless prisoner tempted within by the attractive appearance of a bunch of worms, carefully threaded on a loop of copper wire to prevent their escape between the interstices of the wickerwork. The trap portion of the "leap" is closed at the end by a wooden plug, which can be easily withdrawn to facilitate the despatch of any eels it may contain. A quantity of these wicker traps are baited, and deposited in a boat, and the eel-catcher rows to the place where he intends to set them. Arrived there, he takes up one of them, and fastens it to an old firebar or similar object to act as a sinker, and a few feet of cord buoyed with a huge cork to afford a hold for his boat-hook, when he desires to pick it up again.

Glancing round to mark the situation in his memory, he drops the "leap" overboard, with its entrance facing down-stream, so that eels working up against the stream will have little difficulty in entering the trap. The cork is not allowed to appear on the surface, lest it should offer a clue to unscrupulous individuals who may be prowling about to pick up and empty the trap. But though unseen, it is really necessary, for the sole purpose stated above, namely, that of extending a few feet of cord sufficient to offer a hold for the proprietor's boat-hook on his early morning visits to his fishing grounds.

There are quantities of eels in the Derwent, and plenty of scope for others to take as many as our old wildfowling friend did. He would sometimes work upwards of fifty traps upon one stretch of the water.

Before concluding this chapter, I might describe one or two curious superstitions that pertain to the eel, many rural beliefs being of considerable interest. The mystery surround-ing the birth of the eel is simply explained by the startling and original theory that young eels are evolved from the long hairs shed by horses when down at the ponds to drink ! The first stage of the eel's existence, it is declared, is spent as a "hair-worm" ; and as this is the local name for a creature (Gordius) exactly resembling a living horse-hair, and also found in most stagnant pools, some colour is thereby lent to this popular if absurd belief. According to an old couplet,

> "When the willow comes out in bud,
> Then the eels come out of the mud."

EXAMINING THE
PURSE OF AN
EEL NET.

EMPTYING AN
EEL NET.

Aristotle held the belief that eels were generated in the mud, and Pliny was convinced that each fragment separated from their bodies by friction against a rock, would turn into an eel. Another belief was that eels sprang from May-dew, and that to prove its correctness, one had only to take two pieces of turf covered with dew on a May morning and place them together, grass inwards, when exposure to the heat of the sun would spontaneously generate eels. (Maybe, if left a little longer, they would be stewed ready for the table!)

If any of my readers are interested in the mythology of the eel, they will find some further instances recorded in the Irish Iliad.

CHAPTER XIII.

SOME CONCLUDING REMARKS.

TO a great extent the life of Snowden Slights has been of
the type popularly known as "humdrum." In his
little old-world Yorkshire village the years glide on,
one after another, with a monotonous sameness ; and
days, weeks and months serve but to mark out periods of
time in the existence of its residents. The unlooked-for
advent of a steam roundabout on the occasion of the annual
feast will make quite a sensation, and provide a topic of
conversation for months after, among the simple folk, while
a motor-car has barely ceased to be a novelty.

I have often requested the old wildfowler to cast back in
his memory and relate any incidents of rural life which would
be of interest to-day, but he has confessed himself to be at
a loss for a subject. He remembers, however, occasions
when village life has been quickened by a lively party "riding
the stang," as it was called, in doubtful honour of some
individual who had offended against the local code of morals.
The practice consisted in making an effigy, out of bundles
of straw or other combustible material, to represent the
person whom it was desired to hold up to derision. The
effigy (preferably arrayed in an old suit belonging to the
individual it personated) was placed in a cart or carried upon
a hurdle, and paraded up and down the street in front of
the residence of the luckless rustic. No one was immune

from the probability of being selected as the victim of a "stang riding party." The offence might be grave or quite venial, but no matter—the grocer detected in giving short weight was just as likely to be held up to execration, as a married man discovered making love to a lady other than his wife ; and the man known as a wife-beater was as certain to be thus pilloried, as was one of the opposite sex reported to be a shrew.

After the effigy had been made, it was accompanied to the desired place by a large crowd, one and all trying their hardest to make a terrific noise—singing, shouting, playing accordions and tin whistles, and beating time upon derelict pans, until they were tired of the business, when the effigy was taken into a field and publicly burnt, to the accompaniment of some impromptu ditty suited to the occasion. One of the party would perhaps set a few lines to rhyme, and then fitting them to a popular tune, the rest of the party would join in unison and sing out lustily some such doggerel as this :—

"Ran-a-dan-dan, we ride a stang,
For Tom Jones, whose wife was a-hungered :
When the villain is dead, and his pockets are plundered,
We'll sing o'er him the Old Hundred."

Another rude ditty, evidently intended for a cobbler who had remonstrated rather too roughly with his wife for her carelessness in allowing the kettle to boil dry, and the cakes in the oven to be burnt, runs thus :—

"Ran-a-dan-dan, we ride a stang,
For dirty and brutal Mike Seeley.
The cakes were all burnt and the kettle was dry,
So he up with his leather heel-strap and gave her a black
    eye."

The ditties chosen to be sung on such occasions were invariably coarse and vulgar—several of the wittiest and most rhythmical to such a degree, indeed, that they cannot be reproduced here. Whether or not the fear of being held up to public scorn acted as a deterrent to those who might be contemplating some brutality, I do not know. If it did, the villagers of those days must have been a rather bad lot, as the old man speaks of the practice of "riding the stang" as being a common occurrence.

THE FUTURE OF THE DERWENT VALLEY.

Changes take place slowly in these out-of-the-way districts; for instance, there are no mineral deposits to cause an upheaval when discovered. During the summer, the cattle will still wade knee-deep in the lush grass of the ings, and winter floods will again and again attract the flocks of wildfowl ; but over all there is a suggestion of some subtle change. The advent of the cycle and the motor-car has made these sleepy little villages more accessible than of yore, and a modern railway is to-day pushing its way nearer and nearer until its steel track will almost touch the edge of the solitudes which for generations have been almost indisputably in possession of the wildfowl for six months out of the twelve.

Consequently, the future prospects of wildfowling in the Derwent Valley are not of the brightest. Of necessity, former conditions will have to give way to the more prosperous state of agriculture and the march of improvement which always follows on the heels of the opening of a new line of railway. The new Derwent Valley Light Railway will be almost completed by the time these lines appear in print, and stations at Wheldrake, Thorganby, and Skipwith will afford stopping-places within two or three miles of the principal haunts of the wild life with which the past history of Snowden Slights has been so intimately bound up.

The advent of a denser population, and the fillip given to agricultural interests by cheaper and quicker methods of transit, both of persons and of goods, all tend towards the driving away of creatures that formerly frequented the neighbourhood. Even now, the old-time glories of the river have departed, probably never to return, and to a certain extent it is at present fished out. True, there are yet quantities of fish, but they lack the size and quality that pertained ten years ago. Where there was one follower of the gentle art at that time, there are twenty to-day, and the river does not run which will bear such wholesale depletion as has occurred in the Derwent. Alas! in the coming days, so close at hand, a still greater number of anglers will sit beside the river, and try to lure from its brown depths some of the successors of those grand old specimens which have delighted the hearts of disciples of Walton in the past.

But I must not be too pessimistic. Much of the blame now rests on the now happily passing fishing matches; such gatherings would weigh in anything, from the tiny minnow to the lordly pike, and as at times the party of contestants would muster in hundreds, a considerable amount of reckless spoliation necessarily ensued. The status of the various anglers' clubs has greatly improved of late; their outings do not partake so much of the character of drunken carousals as they used to do, while more careful attention is given to the fixing of minimum sizes at which fish can be taken away when caught; and this, combined with judicious efforts towards re-stocking, is beginning to make itself felt.

While on the subject of fish-depletion, may I appeal to the jaded town worker who looks forward, year by year, to enjoying a well-earned piscatorial holiday? As he drinks in the fine, fresh air, and 'feels himself hourly recuperating whilst watching his float dancing on the stream, let him resolve to render what assistance he can to those who are striving to keep up a good stock of fish for the benefit of future generations.

It behoves every club member who has spent pleasant days with rod and line in the Derwent Valley, to help forward such a good work. True, he cannot do it individually, but he can do it collectively ; for even the smallest fishing club can purchase a few hundred small fish, and see that they are turned into the river in suitable places. Let me conclude by pleading with those who have had their "best times" in this locality, even if years ago, to make it once more possible for others to go and do likewise.

LIST OF SUBSCRIBERS.

Addie, D. Forrester, Bank Chambers, Fleetwood.

Allely, W. S., 3, Regent Street, Birmingham.

Anderson, Dr. Tempest, 17, Stonegate, York.

Baker, E. W., 3, Victoria Crescent, Southsea, Hants.

Black, C., Rectory Farm, Barrow-on-Soar, Leicestershire.

Burdekin, C. L., 35, Parliament Street, York.

Blake, E. C., Hawkshill, Leatherhead.

Benson, Geo., Scarcroft Hill, York.

Blake, Herbert, Tower Cottage, Gosport, Hants.

Boyce, Frank, "Kirkley," Herbert Rd., Hornchurch, Essex.

Clarke, John Talbot, 19, Park Lane, Southwold, Suffolk.

Coffy, Richard B., Garron Lodge, Tyrrellspass, Co. West
Meath.

Cooper, W. A., Selby.

Heath, Charles J., 34, Devonshire Place, London, W.

Hayes, C., 2, Bellevue Road, Southampton.

Higson, Daniel, 63, Waterloo Road, Ashton on Ribble.

Harlock, Sidney, Lapwing Lane, W. Didsbury, Manchester.

Halkes, John W., The Limes, 141, Monk's Road, Lincoln.

Hewertson, James, Clappersgate, Ambleside, Westmorland.

Houseman, H., Grange Street, Fulford Road, York.

Higson, Athelstan, 8, Station Rd., Harborne, Birmingham.

Hillier, William Iles, The Firs, King's Caple, Hereford.

Gower, Thos. B., 14, Ontario Terrace, Rathmines, Dublin.

Gallwey, Bart., Sir Ralph Payne, Thirkleby Park, Thirsk, Yorkshire.

Gill, Harold, The Warrens, Parkgate, Cheshire.

Grabham, M.A., Oxley, The Museum, York.

Gray, T., Straker's Passage, Fossgate, York.

Greenwood, Major Joseph, 8, Clifton Dale, York.

Dunnington-Jefferson, J. J., Thicket Priory, York.

Dockray, John A., Gayton Cottage, Heswall, Cheshire.

Dutton, Robert, 15, Davygate, York.

Duncan, Stanley, 44, De la Pole, Anlaby Road, Hull.

Elmhirst, Charles Ernest, 29, Mount Vale, York.

Etheridge, Ernest, Ringwood, Hants.

Evans, William, 5, Gelli Street, Caeran, nr. Bridgend.

Everitt, Nicholas, Oulton Broad, Lowestoft.

Ellicott, W., 20, Cambrian Road, Richmond, Surrey.

Fox, W., 64, Wigginton Road, York.

Jones, H. J., Hope Villa, Huntington Road, York.

Leonard, Reginald H., 4, The Avenue, Clifton, York.

Kelschendorf, Baron de, Hemingford Abbots, St. Ives, Hunts.

Kirk, G. W., Appledene, East Parade, York.

Mayne, Dr. W. Boxer, Swindon.

Moxon, Arthur H., 94, Rocky Lane, Monton, near Manchester.

Monkton, Arthur Reginald, 103, Wallwood Road, Leytonstone, N.E.

Mathews, Frank, The Grove, Woodhey, Rock Ferry, Cheshire.

Mennell, John, 27, Neville Street, York.

Oates, Fredk. William, White House Farm, New Leeds, Leeds.

Pennington, Douglas (Wildfowlers' Executive Committee), Lancaster House, Birkdale, Southport.

Peace, R. A., Broadwood, Maghull, nr. Liverpool.

Phillips, E. Cambridge (President, Woolhope Naturalists' Field Club, Hereford), Brooklands, Hay, via Hereford.

Purcell, L., Severn View, Saul, Glos.

Philip, Son and Nephew, Ltd., South Castle St., Liverpool.

Sharpe, Edmund, Halton Hall, Lancaster.

Snell, W., Fore Street, Redruth.

Story, Edwin, Micklegate, York.

Stott, Geo. H., Old George Hotel, York.

Scarr, Stanley, Folk Hall, New Earswick, York.

Stansfield, H., 20, Park Grove, York.

Skilbeck, H., 9, Neville Terrace, York.

Rose, M., 19, Woodheyes Road, London, N.W.

Room, George, 50, Pasture Road, Harehills Avenue, Leeds.

Roberts, T. N., 38, West Bank, Scarborough.

Rogers, Leonard B., Welton Dale, Brough, E. Yorks.

Tattersall, F., 34, Penley's Grove Street, York.

Yorkshire Philosophical Society, The Museum, York.

Waddington, Thos. Fairbank, Moor-Allerton, Leeds.

Zimmerman, V. G. F., 7, Portland Street, York.

SCHULTZE
POWDER. :

Illustrated Sporting and Dramatic News.

Established 1874.

SATURDAY—PRICE SIXPENCE.

A NEWSPAPER FOR TOWN AND COUNTRY.

The ILLUSTRATED SPORTING AND DRAMATIC NEWS contains numerous engravings of sporting, dramatic, and general subjects, by eminent artists ; and is one of the best illustrated journals of the day.

The letterpress is bright, entertaining, and original, and treats of hunting, coursing, racing, golf, rowing, fishing, athletics, and all field sports ; the drama, music, literature, agriculture, and every topic likely to interest the country gentleman and general public.

A Special edition on thin paper is published weekly, to suit the foreign postal rates.

TERMS OF SUBSCRIPTION.

INLAND (POST FREE).

	£	s.	d.
12 Months (including Xmas No.)	1	8	0
6 ,, ...	0	14	0
3 ,, ...	0	7	0

A Special Edition is printed on thin paper, and forwarded post free to any part of the World at the rate of :—

	£	s.	d.
12 Months (including Xmas No.)	1	16	0
6 ,, ...	0	18	8

Xmas No. 1s. 4d. extra.
All Subscriptions payable in advance.

Post Office Orders to be made payable to Mr. G. J. MADDICK, at the East Strand Post Office. Cheques crossed "Bank of England," Law Court Branch.

Offices : 172, STRAND, LONDON, W.C.

A Thrilling Tale ! !

TOM LEE:

A WHARFEDALE TRAGEDY

By Heather Bell.

GRASSINGTON BRIDGE.

Threepence : All Booksellers.   By Post, 4½d.

York:

Printed and Published by T. A. J. Waddington,
Mansfield Street, Foss Islands.

The Abbeys and Castles of Yorkshire

ILLUSTRATED.

PRICE **1/-**

T. A J. WADDINGTON, Publisher, Mansfield Street, YORK.

Waddington's Guides.

Morecambe and Lancaster—40 p.p., with Map. One Penny.

York and its Minster—104 p.p., with Plan. One Penny.

Scarborough and Filey—64 p.p., Illustrated. One Penny.

Where Shall We Go For A Holiday?—Walking Tours in the Yorkshire Dales and Lakeland. By "A Son of the Soil." With Plates. 48 p.p. Twopence.

Ilkley and Bolton Abbey—48 p.p. One Penny.

Bridlington and Flamborough—40 p.p. One Penny.

Lancaster Castle Illustrated, 64 p.p. One Penny.

The North of Ireland and Giant's Causeway—Twopence.

Belfast, Co. Down, and the Mourne Mountains—48 p.p., Illustrated with Maps, Plans, etc. Twopence.

Donegal Highlands—Twopence.

Dublin and Killarney—64 p.p., Well Illustrated. Twopence.

York—200 p.p., Maps, Plans, etc. Sixpence.

Londonderry and Donegal Highlands—48 p.p. Threepence.

Around and About Morecambe Bay—From Fleetwood to Barrow in-Furness. Illustrated with Maps, Plans, etc. A Most Complete Guide. Sixpence.

Furness Abbey and District—40 p.p., One Penny.

Grange-over-Sands, Arnside, and Silverdale—40 p.p., One Penny.

Windermere and Grasmere—32 p.p., One Penny.

Lakeland—Excursions in the Lake District, by "A Son of the Soil."—48 p.p., Well Illustrated on Art Paper Threepence.

Kirkby Lonsdale—64 p.p., Illustrated. One Penny.

Redcar and Saltburn—32 p.p., Illustrated and Map of Golf Links One Penny.

Saltburn and Staithes—32 p.p., Illustrated. One Penny.

Day Drives in the Craven Dales—48 p.p., Illustrated and Driving Map. A Most Complete Guide. Threepence.

Llandudno, In and Around—32 p.p., Well Illustrated, with Plan of the Town. One Penny

Kirkstall Abbey—32 p.p., Plan of the Abbey. One Penny

Grassington—104 p.p., Illustrated. Twopence.

St. Mary's Abbey, York—40 p.p., Illustrated Twopence.

The Abbeys and Castles of Yorkshire—200 p.p., Illustrated. One Shilling. .

Lancaster—64 p.p. Twopence.

Lancaster—40 p.p., Illustrated. One Penny.

Selby Abbey and Howden Church—Twopence.

On Sale at all Stationers and Bookstalls, or Post Free from—

T. A. J. WADDINGTON, Publisher, YORK.

Waddington's Sixpenny Guide.

IN AND AROUND

MORECAMBE

AND

ITS BAY,

INCLUDING LAKE WINDERMERE CIRCULAR TOUR.

THE BEST GUIDE.

On Sale at all Booksellers and Bookstalls in the District.